Future Proof
INVESTING

Kelly Gilbert
Steve Kitchen

Black Lake Press
TELL YOUR STORY
BLACKLAKEPRESS.COM

Illustrations and graphics by Jessica Newton.
Cover design by Courtney Van De Burg.
Senior editor: Cory Lakatos.
Published by Black Lake Press of
Holland, Michigan.

Black Lake Press is a division of
Black Lake Studio, LLC.
Direct inquiries to Black Lake Press at
www.blacklakepress.com.
ISBN 978-0-9883373-8-1

DEDICATION

Kelly:
I dedicate this book to my wife Ronda, who has been my biggest supporter and encourager for over thirty years. She is my Proverbs 31:10 wife.

Steve:
I dedicate this book to my wife Julie and my kids Haley, Hillary, and Little Rudy (AKA Riley), who love it when dad is home, but still put up with my seemingly endless hours of entrepreneurial work and dedication. I also dedicate this book to Ted and Sherry Kitchen, who taught me the value of working hard and that you can achieve anything you dedicate yourself to.

TABLE OF CONTENTS

Acknowledgements

We would like to thank all of our clients, who over the years have put their trust in us to help them create and design a more successful financial future. We have shared many of life's ups and downs, and we are blessed to have known all of you. These relationships helped us to gain the wisdom, knowledge, and courage to write this book. Because of you, many other business owners, professionals, retirees, and pre-retires can also find a lasting solution to achieving their financial goals.

We would also like to thank everyone who has contributed and helped us to complete this book. We always joke that good ideas are plentiful, but flawless execution is priceless, and without your help, this book might have never been completed.

PREFACE

In the early nineteenth century the art of weather predicting was considered a form of witchcraft. That may seem silly nowadays with our satellite photos, weather maps, and the plethora of meteorologists on TV, but none of those things existed back then. Predicting weather was more akin to calling a psychic hotline than it was to science. Back then and still today, without empirical evidence, predictions about the future are almost always wrong. And even with all his resources today, our local weatherman is still wrong sometimes.

By the same token, if you track the collective performance of the current batch of financial gurus and MSNBC talking heads over the last ten to fifteen years, it is baffling how much confidence they still lay claim to. But let's not be so hard on them just yet. Human beings have always been attracted to predictions and forecasts. And as long as there is a willing audience, the performers and marketers will always be there to profit from it.

So what is Future Proof investing? Let's start with what it is not. It is not a new attempt to predict where the stock market will go. It is not a new mathematical algorithm to predict which investments to buy or sell. It is not a psychic hotline.

Future Proof investing is a process that enables investors to slowly and intelligently gravitate away from gambling with their financial future. The process helps the investor to replace risks with guarantees and substitute predictable growth and safety where overly conservative decisions have created unintended losses. The overriding mantra of Future Proof investing is to plan and create an attainable and sustainable financial future.

The Future Proof process is a layered and iterative approach. This means it starts at the top layer and carefully works participants down to the core components at a predictable path and reasonable pace.

The starting point is to simply answer the following four questions logically and truthfully. These four questions are the only future predictions required to Future Proof your investments.

1. **On the day you plan to start your retirement, do you believe that taxes will be higher or lower than they are today?** This is an extremely important question for anyone's financial future, as taxation is the number one wealth risk known to man.

2. **Have you calculated the income you'll need in retirement, adjusted for inflation?** In other words, have you taken into account that in fifteen, twenty, or thirty years your current income level might be the new poverty level due to inflation?

3. **Will you outlive your money during retirement?** This could be the most important question of the four, and it has risen to the forefront in recent years because the typical Baby Boomer is now expected to live well into their eighties or nineties, or even older.

4. **What do you wish for your heirs after you pass away?** Do you plan on providing an inheritance for your children and your children's children?

Preface

By simply answering these four questions logically and truthfully, not emotionally or with politically correct idioms, you can begin the process of Future Proofing your finances.

While these questions seem obvious, many Americans have either chosen or been led to ignore them. This book will help you honestly answer these questions and then apply the results to your financial plans.

In this book we will use a hypothetical mission to Mars as a symbolic representation of your retirement journey. You will read how investing for your retirement is a lot like planning a Mars mission: it seems impossibly far away, and there are all kinds of potential dangers and unknown threats. There's an abundance of misinformation about what your destination is like and the best way to get there. And once you arrive, you have to figure out how to survive on nothing but the supplies you brought with you. So how are you going to Future Proof your investments? As your mission planners, we will show you how to dodge the pitfalls and make a plan for an attainable and sustainable future.

CHAPTER 1

MYTHS AND MISTAKEN MODELS

Mankind has always looked up at the sky with longing. From the time of the ancient Greeks and Romans we have pointed our eyes and our telescopes upward and dreamed of making a home on another world. The red planet especially has captured our imaginations. Its similarities to Earth and relative closeness to us in the solar system have made it an attractive option for our first foray into the colonization of space. But even Mars seemed hopelessly distant. How could we possibly reach it? And if we got there, how would we survive?

As time passed, the lack of solid information led to all manner of myths cropping up about the red

AS LONG AS MAN HAS WALKED THE EARTH, HE HAS DREAMED OF REACHING MARS, BUT IT HAS ALWAYS SEEMED IMPOSSIBLY DISTANT.

planet. People said it was a dangerous world of harsh, dry deserts punctuated by swiftly flowing rivers and canals. It was inhabited by all manner of hostile alien creatures. Mars, we were told, was an unfriendly, inhospitable place. Most despaired of ever reaching it, let alone finding a way to live there. Those who didn't give up based their plans on wild rumors and misinformation.

However, as science marched forward in the twentieth century, mankind suddenly had a much more accurate picture of conditions on Mars. Probes brought back soil samples and images of the surface, dispelling the myths we had long believed. Advances in technology made the idea of sending a manned mission to the red *planet realistic. At the dawn of the twenty-first century, mankind looks to the sky with confidence that one day soon they would plant their first colony on Mars.*

Investing for your retirement is a lot like mankind's quest to colonize the red planet. We all aspire to retire with enough financial assets to live comfortably, but that goal often seems out of reach. Not only is it a distant goal, depending on your age, but it's one fraught with risk. How will you put away enough? What investments will get you there? Once you get there, how do you make sure the money doesn't run out before you die? What if taxes go up or the stock market crashes? What will you do then?

ALL MANNER OF MYTHS PREVAILED ABOUT THE RED PLANET. MANKIND DESPAIRED OF EVER REACHING THIS MYSTERIOUS, DANGEROUS WORLD.

BUT RECENT RESEARCH HAS DISPELLED THE MISCONCEPTIONS, REVEALING MARS TO BE WITHIN OUR REACH. WITH PROPER PLANNING, MAN CAN MAKE THE RED PLANET HOME.

There are many people who will try to help you answer those questions, but myths and misinformation abound. Much of the conventional wisdom is based on outdated or inaccurate models. You might think you've got it figured out, but what if you're operating on unreliable information?

But just as new discoveries and new technologies could make a manned mission to Mars a reality in the near future, so too are new research and new methods— and rediscovered, tried-and-true methods from the past—making your secure retirement possible. With accurate advice and proper planning, you can invest in a Future Proof retirement.

Anyone reading recent financial articles or magazines will surely notice the plethora of retirement articles lamenting the fact that 401(k) retirement plans are falling well short of expectations. We are constantly reminded of the financial havoc that recent market downturns have wreaked on an unsuspecting public. While everyone agrees that the government qualified (and regulated) 401(k)/IRA path to retirement has been a dismal failure for most Americans, they are still being referred to as "retirement savings plans." In fact, it rarely takes more than two sentences for these stock market authors and pundits to use the term "savings plan" as they describe stock and bond portfolios that have lost large percentages of value.

This leads us to our foundational proof statement for a Future Proof investor: Any savings account that is exposed to stock market risks is not a retirement savings account! It never has been and never will be. Exposure to market risks makes it a securities investment at risk of total loss, not a retirement savings plan! For many of our readers, this statement is both obvious and confusing at the same time. It's obvious that a stock and bond portfolio can experience losses, while confusing because we have been programmed to believe that these portfolios are the best place to "save" for retirement.

Let's explore this further by asking ourselves some simple questions. How is it that we so easily confuse securities-based investments (risky) with retirement savings (safe)! Aren't we always told that if you cannot afford to lose it all, then do not take the risk? And how many of us can afford another "Lost Decade"? Isn't this just common sense? But simply take a look around you at all the examples of brokerage house marketing and U.S. government propaganda. Americans have been programmed to ignore the fact that their government-qualified IRA and 401(k) retirement plans are stock market risk plans, not safe and steadily growing retirement savings plans. Wall Street is notorious for using hypothetical compound interest calculations to show us how much money we can make over twenty years using a 9% "average" stock market return. Now ask yourself, who has made an actual 9% investment gain every year? Who has even averaged 9%? So how can Wall Street be allowed to use a "constant interest rate" in their investment and savings examples? It always amazes us how obviously dangerous this appears when exposed, yet how oblivious some investors are to it. In fact, whenever we articulate this at cocktail parties or events, we feel like the boy who accused the emperor of having no clothes. If you are wondering if you might be one of the millions of Americans who have been duped into this high stakes gambit, do not dismay just yet, because it's not all your fault—but after you read this book, that may change.

Let's look at how it all started. Prior to the 1980s, a proper, government-approved financial pyramid instructed Americans to keep 80% of their money in safe, liquid, and income-generating financial vehicles. This left only 20% of exposed to systematic risk in stocks, bonds, real estate, and other risk-based

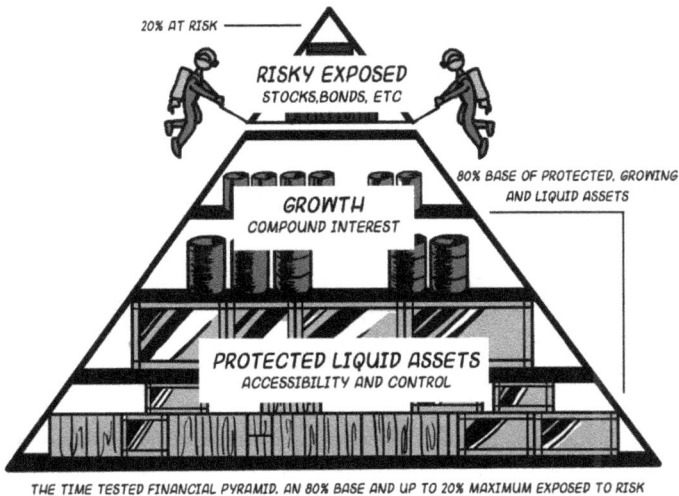

20% AT RISK

RISKY EXPOSED
STOCKS,BONDS, ETC

80% BASE OF PROTECTED, GROWING
AND LIQUID ASSETS

GROWTH
COMPOUND INTEREST

PROTECTED LIQUID ASSETS
ACCESSIBILITY AND CONTROL

THE TIME TESTED FINANCIAL PYRAMID. AN 80% BASE AND UP TO 20% MAXIMUM EXPOSED TO RISK investments. Then came the 1978 and 1980 amended section 401(k) laws that enacted and enabled 401(k) s and Individual Retirement Accounts (IRAs) which we will call government-qualified accounts or qualified accounts. This drew money out of the interest-bearing, safe, and sometimes tax-favored savings accounts and into the stock market with tax-deferred and risk-exposed investment vehicles. This created more potential tax revenue (good for the IRS) and more money in the stock market (good for the businesses that fuel our economy), but what did it do for the American public? For the next twenty years or so the stock market rose steadily because millions of blue-collar workers gave up their pensions and began "saving" in stock and bond portfolios instead. By the late 90s, after years of relentless propaganda

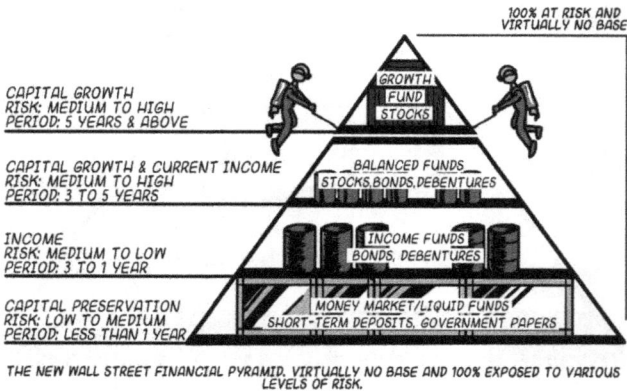

THE NEW WALL STREET FINANCIAL PYRAMID. VIRTUALLY NO BASE AND 100% EXPOSED TO VARIOUS LEVELS OF RISK.

from Wall Street and the IRS, the previous sane advice of maintaining 80% of your money outside the stock market was deemed lunacy and downright crazy talk.

Then came the tech bubble burst of 2000, followed by the 9/11 downturn in 2001, and then the "Great Recession" of 2007. The last thing anyone expects now is a constantly rising stock market like the 80s and 90s enjoyed. In fact, most agree that the stock market is now a never-ending roller coaster ride. All the investment and retirement savings theories that were developed during the up years now require a complete

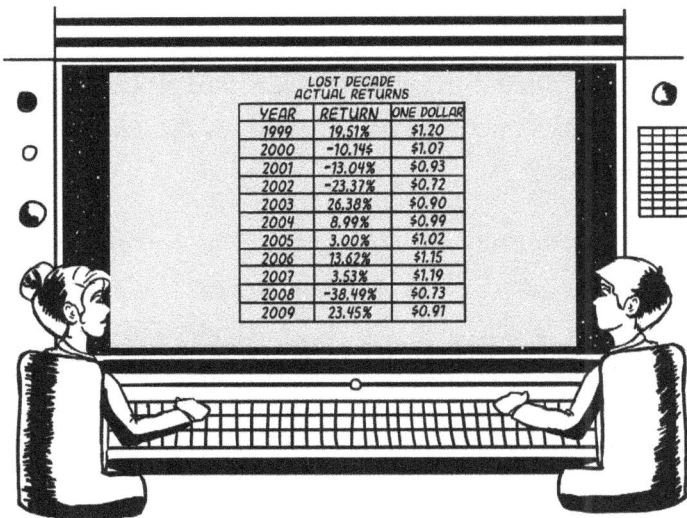

LOST DECADE
ACTUAL RETURNS

YEAR	RETURN	ONE DOLLAR
1999	19.51%	$1.20
2000	-10.14%	$1.07
2001	-13.04%	$0.93
2002	-23.37%	$0.72
2003	26.38%	$0.90
2004	8.99%	$0.99
2005	3.00%	$1.02
2006	13.62%	$1.15
2007	3.53%	$1.19
2008	-38.49%	$0.73
2009	23.45%	$0.91

overhaul to avoid certain failure. But tragically, most Americans have been trained to cling to the old axioms of a "diversified portfolio," "buy and hold," or "long-term investing" as the only way to manage risk and grow their retirement savings plan. The unfortunate result is millions of Americans suffering 20-40% losses from which they may never recover.

So why do the majority of Americans still blindly follow the obviously flawed retirement advice of Wall Street and the IRS? That is a good question that cries out for a good answer! By now you're probably thinking, "Where else can your retirement savings grow faster than inflation without losses and risks?" The answer existed long ago, prior to the 1978 401(k) amendment. But sadly, after thirty years of Wall Street advice and propaganda, Americans no longer know the truth about their money.

A Future Proof investor knows that to truly create wealth, your money must work for you 24/7/365 in a tax-medicated vehicle that provides guarantees to preserve your principal investment amounts. In other words, you need compound interest growth with zero losses. This implies three simple Future Proofing rules:

1. The only way to grow your life savings is through compound interest, and compound interest is not available in the stock market.

2. Your gains must also be as free from taxation as possible; otherwise you will lose money 24/7. Tax-deferred is not tax-free—it is tax-delayed, and if your tax rates go up (which they always seem to do), then tax-deferred becomes a "tax-increased" savings plan.

3. Protecting your principal means that your life savings account value will never go below your initial deposit(s) amount(s). This is strike three for Wall Street. Wall Street money is always exposed to risk and there is no guarantee that you will not lose it all.

So what are your remaining options? The IRS and Wall Street have trained Americans to think that the only alternative to their risk-exposed stocks and bonds is their evil twin, the banks. The banks offer savings accounts that preserve your capital—that is, until they take out all their newly designed fees. And the interest rate on most savings accounts is zero, not to mention the fact that the IRS charges you high taxes on any gains you may get from these bank savings accounts. So much for Future Proofing rules two and three.

But what about CDs, or certificates of deposit? CDs get an interest rate that is higher than savings or checking accounts, so this satisfies rule one of working for you 24/7/365. But today that rate is so low that the risky stock market begins to look good again. And how does a CD fare in the taxation area? Taxation of CDs is always at the current capital gains rate and is calculated annually, with no deferral like stocks offer. Thus, your annual interest gains are systematically reduced by the current capital gains tax rate. No advantage here for the bank. But what about rule three, safety and avoiding losses? Yes, CDs satisfy rule three. If you put $1,000 into a five-year CD, you have some guarantees that your original $1,000 will still be there when you come back. Of course, the interest gained may not be enough to outpace inflation, but we will discuss that at length in later chapters.

Now let's review how most of America has been trained by our bankers, IRS agents, and Wall Street brokers. It might be summarized by saying that our only option is a balanced portfolio of stocks and bonds, and if you are really adverse to the risks involved, you can put some money in a CD that makes almost nothing in interest, or a savings/checking/money market account that gives you even less interest but is liquid, readily available, and preserves your capital.

If you are nodding your head yes right now and wondering if there is anything outside of what was just detailed, you are not alone. In fact, we estimate that the majority of Americans are right there with you. And this partially explains why so many Americans are in so much financial trouble when it comes to retirement plans and their life savings accounts.

Now for the good news: this book will attempt to reintroduce you to a financial strategy that a growing number of Americans are shifting large portions of their life savings back into. These strategies adhere to all three of the Future Proofing wealth creation rules. These retirement savings secrets are obvious yet obscure, because they fly in the face of the Wall Street propaganda and marketing machines. Like a voice in the wilderness, we state loudly that a retirement savings plan that exposes most of it's money to stock market risks is a bad plan. We further contend that a proper plan maintains approximately 80% of your financial assets in safe, protected, and income-generating vehicles and leaves

Chapter 1: Myths and Mistaken Models

only a small percentage exposed to stock market risks. If you do this correctly, your savings will grow steadily and you can avoid being a bad retirement savings example for some magazine article. Or maybe we are lunatics, just as your stock broker and banker contend. But unlike them, we will let you decide.

CHAPTER 2

FUNDS, FUELS, AND THE FUTURE

Before you can build a colony on the red planet, you have to figure out how you're going to get there. One of the first decisions faced by mission control is coming up with a fuel strategy that will get the crew to their new home on Mars.

There are three different schools of thought on this puzzle. Some experts recommend a fuel called RAPTOR X-3, a volatile, high-yield propellant. There's no fuel on the market that provides a higher speed with less weight, meaning you can build a sleeker, lighter, and faster rocket. RAPTOR X-3 gives you the most bang for your buck, but the unstable nature of the liquid means that the tiniest problem could cause the whole ship to

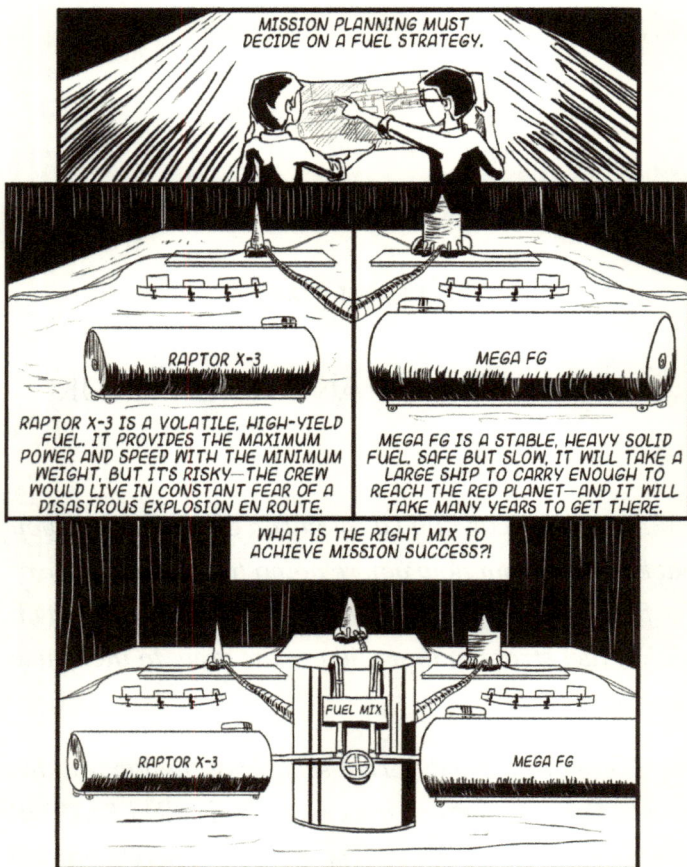

explode. If even a minuscule asteroid clips the hull, or if the mission's engineers make the slightest mistake in the engine room, your colony could blow up in your face before it's ever planted.

Other scientists suggest MEGA FG, a stable but heavy fuel. Your rocket would have to be weightier, larger, and slower, but it would be substantially safer. However, it would take a massive amount of this solid fuel to reach the red planet, and it could take lifetimes to do so. Plus, the expense involved in stockpiling that much fuel is all but cost-prohibitive.

The third camp posits that the best way to get to Mars is to mix the two fuels, thereby getting the benefits and overcoming the drawbacks of both. Your ship could be mid-sized and fly at a reasonable speed without quite as much risk. But within this camp there is disagreement about the right proportions of RAPTOR X-3 and MEGA FG to use.

You'll face similar challenges when deciding how to invest your money. You could put it in the stock market, but that opens you up to a lot of risk—your retirement savings could go up in smoke at any time. You could opt to put it in bank accounts and CDs, but you'll have to stockpile an awful lot of cash without much help from interest. Conventional wisdom says to balance your portfolio with stocks, bonds, bank accounts, and CDs, but is that really enough to attain a retirement fund that's sustainable?

Chapter 2: Funds, Fuels, and the Future

Let's begin with the volatile fuel, the stock market. How volatile is it, really? Let's assume for a minute that you wanted to give us $500,000 of your retirement funds. In return for this large portion of your retirement nest egg, all you expect is a meaningful and predictable return on the investment. But before we accept the money from you, we require you to sign a binding contract which states that you could lose all your money due to systematic risks that are outside of our control, and if you do lose your money, you have no legal recourse against us or our company. We would also require you to acknowledge that there is no guarantee that you will ever make any money on the investment while it is in our control. Would you sign that form and entrust us with your retirement nest egg? Would anyone? Would you do it if we showed you all the professional accreditations we have? Would you sign if we told you that everyone else was doing it? Would you sign it if we told you that our company is very big and old? If you knew us personally that might help, but if you had never met us before, would you trust us after we required you to sign that contract?

As absurd as this may sound, it is interesting to us how hundreds of thousands of people sign that very form/contract every day when they buy a mutual fund or open up an IRA, 401(k), or college 529 plan. That's right—before you can put money into a stock or bond, you must sign a contract that acknowledges the fact that you're exposing your money to risk and could lose it all, that you have no guarantee of gains, and that you waive your legal rights on these losses or gains. We would venture to guess that most people don't even read this contract. They just sign on the dotted line and blindly trust the broker or banker who is selling to them. We know how easily it can happen because we have both unwittingly signed a few over the years. The fact is that we opened 401(k)s and IRAs back in the 1980s, and we even participated in employee stock purchase plans back in the 90s (fortunately they were not the Enron employee stock purchase plans). Looking back on it, we assume that we must have just trusted the brokerage firms (being sponsored by an employer helped establish this trust), and we simply thought that everybody else was doing it, so it must be alright.

What is the history behind this form/contract that every investor must sign? It grew out of the 1978 IRS 401(k) mandate that enabled employers to exit pension retirement planning and shift all the risk to their employees and participants.

This also created a need for the U.S. Security and Exchange Commission (SEC) to mandate a process to "protect" investors from less than honest stock brokers. The process states that every stockbroker is required to walk you through a survey that they call a risk tolerance questionnaire. The goal of this process is to somehow ascertain your investment risk tolerance level. While there is no standard scale or rating, the usual levels are high, moderate, and low, or aggressive, growth, and income. But the stock broker asking the questions must use your answers to decide where you are on his scale, and then every stock or bond that he sells you must somehow be tied to your category/level. Once a portfolio has been designed to match your tolerance level, this "Understanding of Risk" form/contract must be signed as the last step before exposing your funds to risks and losses. The SEC originally created this system to protect the consumer, but over the years the level of subjectivity that each brokerage firm can legally induce, coupled with the protection they get when you sign the contract/form absolving them of any liability, has created a true "buyer beware" scenario. But hey, everyone is doing it, so it must be OK, right?

Now that you know why they require the contract and the questionnaire, let's talk about the axiom that almost all stock brokers use to sell their stocks and bonds: "risk and reward." They almost always imply that in order to get bigger gains (rewards), one must take on bigger risks. But who is taking the risks? It is always you, not your broker. And the rewards are never guaranteed to you, but they are guaranteed to the broker in the way of fees, which are dutifully deducted from your account. Whether you make money or lose money, your brokers always get their fees! This fee constant is commonly referred to as the "spread." It is the difference between your gains and their fees. Spread is just another one of the confusing Wall Street terms from an industry that has a tendency to create a language all its own. In the next few paragraphs we will attempt to explain "Wall Street words" in layman's terms.

For instance, the word "market" typically refers to the stock markets and bond markets as a whole. The market performance may be represented by several different indexes. Indexes may best be understood by the old saying that "all ships rise and fall equally with the tide." Market indexes are very good indicators of the tide rising or falling within that market segment. Indexes like the S&P 500, Dow Jones Industrial Average, Russell 2000, or Barclay's Aggregate Bond Index, to name a few, are used to measure the changes in specific areas of the financial markets. Indexes are referred to as benchmarks against which many investments, such as mutual funds, try to measure themselves. These indexes use a theoretical portfolio of selected stocks or bonds that are related to the financial market or economic segment that they try to measure. One cannot actually invest in an index, but index mutual funds, futures, and exchange-traded funds are used by investors who want to try to buy into the "market" as a whole and within a particular segment of a market.

Now that you have an idea of what the market and market indexes are, let's go back a step and talk about the difference between stocks and bonds. Stocks are shares of a private company that are sold in order to raise money for the corporation. When you buy a stock, you become a partial owner of that company. If the company does well, then your ownership portion is now worth more if someone were to buy it from you. When a company is doing well, many investors want to buy their stock, so they begin bidding at prices that are sometimes higher than the stock should be worth. This artificially inflates the price of the stock because of limited supply and growing demand.

Conversely, if the company falters, many investors will try to sell to a now limited pool of buyers. Thus, they lower their price to try and get rid of it. These upward and downward price fluctuations are what we refer to as stock market risks because these fluctuations should only be driven by real world company valuation changes, but many times they are triggered by emotional responses, as in the case of the 1929 crash. Other times it is because of computerized selling gone haywire, such as the 1984 correction. Still others are because the entire stock market took a big hit, such as the 2001 crash after the 9/11 tragedy or the 2007 mortgage and derivatives debacles.

The bond market, which is larger than the stock market, is a bit different. The bond market is where debt obligations are sold in order to raise money. A debt obligation in the form of a note is issued by an entity which could be a corporation or government body. The issuer guarantees the bond and promises to pay interest on a regular basis to the note (bond) holders. Thus, we have bond market risk, because if the bondholder were to default on that debt, you would lose all your money.

There is also risk because as interest rates rise and fall, bond holders are trying to buy and sell notes similar to the fluctuations that stocks suffer from.

These two aspects of risk (stock risk and bond risk) make up the bulk of what we refer to as market risks. Wall Street calls the risk or uncertainty associated within the entire market "systematic risk" (sometimes referred to as "systemic risk"). In other words, investing in either market is uncertain at all times. Systematic risk is why the SEC mandates that no one can ever say that they "know" where the market is headed. Systematic risk implies that uncertainty is deep-seated in the market. It moves up and down with a regularity that cannot be anticipated! For the casual or amateur investor, systematic risk can be very problematic.

Not surprisingly, Wall Street has figured out a way to measure the risk associated with the market. They then use this measurement to legally absolve themselves of losses after you purchase the stock or bond, because they say it is within your "risk tolerance" level. This measurement is called "volatility." They measure volatility by looking at the historical returns of a stock or index and then plot them on a graph. Then they look to see how scattered or condensed the dots are over time. The further apart the dots are on the graph, the higher the volatility, and the higher the volatility, the riskier the investment. This is how brokers score stocks to fit within the risk tolerance levels that were chosen in your questionnaire. We have done many risk tolerance questionnaires, and as you can probably guess, most investors score towards the conservative end of the spectrum. Very few are aggressive and embrace risk. Wall Street knows this, and this is where an old standby and a relatively new invention come in: bonds and mutual funds.

If you look at the volatility measurement process and apply that measurement to bonds, you can easily expect that since bonds are connected to interest rate changes, the dots on the graph will be relatively close together, and volatility will therefore be very low. Thus, any investor should buy some bonds, right? But as we said before, bonds have inherent bond risk associated with them. While they are not volatile, they are always at risk—systematic risk! The quality of a bond is only as good as the quality of the company or government entity that is issuing the bond. If you had bought Enron or Bear Stearns bonds, then you would have lost all your money. Also note that bonds lose value in a rising interest rate climate. Thus, owning a bond when interest rates are at an all-time low is risky because the only place rates can go is up. Bonds also expose your money to systematic risk because we cannot predict when interest rates and inflation will rise. But if history is any indication, it will happen, and the bond market will drop.

The second legal and SEC-approved saleable item for the investor who scored near the moderate risk levels might be the "mutual fund". A mutual fund (Wall Street recently shortened the name to "fund" with a descriptive name in front such as "growth fund' or "bond fund") is a collection of individual stocks owned by a group and managed by a fund manager. The idea is that if one stock goes down, there are many other stocks that might stay flat or go up to offset the loss—hence the original name "mutual," which describes the original group concept of insurance. The SEC approved the mutual fund in the mid-1980s. Prior to that, only individual stocks or bonds could be sold to consumers. The hype around mutual funds was that they were a surefire way to protect your money while still beating the market. But the 2001 market drop proved once again that systematic risk cannot be removed. During the last ten to thirteen years, mutual funds have rarely kept pace with the index benchmarks that they were supposed to beat. In fact, the average mutual fund return is widely accepted to be 2% below the average stock market performance. From 2002 to 2012 the S&P 500 produced an average rate of return of 3.058%, but during this same period of time the mutual fund actual returns were only 1.02%.[1]

The other downfall for the mutual fund investor is the spread issue. Mutual funds always charge fees. The fund manager and sometimes the brokerage house collect their fees whether the fund gains or loses. This can create a drag on any gains within the fund and can cause accelerated losses during down periods.

Now let's look at the stock, bond, and mutual fund markets as a whole, as well as their most recent history. Their performance can be best summarized by an editorial from Investment Advisor Magazine back in July of 2009. The advisor was commenting on the market collapse of 2008 and 2009. He made this point about Wall Street and the diversification models being used and how they failed their largest test ever: "fixed income substitutes pushed by the major investment houses, low volatility hedge funds, preferred stocks, asset-backed

---

1   Matt Deaton and Damon Roberts, "Average Return: Wall Street's Dirty Little Secret," *FOX Business*, August 12, 2013, www.foxbusiness.com.

securities or other structured products, closed-end bond funds, income/mortgage REITs, and master limited partnerships weren't fixed income substitutes at all. None of them are a substitute for the most important characteristic that investors should be looking for from the fixed income portion of their portfolios; safety of principal..."

Bank or Bury?

Now that we have discussed the volatile fuels of Wall Street, let's look at the banking industry and their solutions, which we deemed MEGA FG, a stable but heavy fuel. Stable and safe are the desired characteristics here, and if safety of principal and protection from losses cannot be achieved with the volatile fuels of the stock and bond markets, no matter how hard you try, where can you preserve your capital when safety and moderation is desired? When pushed, most brokers and bankers will tell you that the only way you can do that is by using bank-based financial vehicles such as savings accounts and CDs. These banking devices are also recommended by Wall Street and banks when an investor insists on having some liquidity for nearly instantaneous access to his or her money. Many types of savings and checking accounts have been created to do just that.

Savings accounts do hold your money in safe and available limbo, but unfortunately they provide you with zero interest. In fact, we have been trained to accept that because bank savings and checking accounts are liquid and available, we shouldn't expect any gains or potential returns. But a sensible axiom about money is that "your money should never sleep." This implies that any accumulated funds should be growing 24/7/365 through compound interest or gains. Unfortunately for most, if you have your money in a bank savings or checking account, your bank is making interest on your money as they lend it out to others, but you do not get any of those gains. Thus, your money is fast asleep. It is available and liquid, and perhaps that makes you feel better, but there is a better way. We'll get into that in greater detail later in this book.

Bank-based savings accounts, checking accounts, and money market accounts are generally accepted as carriers of money for short-term goals. Examples are vacations, buying a car, your daughter's wedding, your child's next tuition payment, a new furnace, etc. Also, traditional wisdom suggests that you keep six to twelve months' salary available in case you experience interruptions in your income streams due to job loss or disability. Short-term needs dictate quick access, and you expect no strings attached in the form of penalties for early withdrawals. The alternative funding for a short-term need would be to liquidate a long-term asset at a time when it may mean a sizable financial loss to do so because of market fluctuations. Imagine that your daughter wanted to get married in 2008 when your mutual funds were at an all-time low. Cashing out then would not have been the best idea, and that is why some liquid, short-term money is a very good plan. But while bank savings and checking accounts do offer easy accessibility (liquidity), they are by far the least profitable place to put your money. In fact, if you are not careful, their drastically increased fee structures can even eat away at your principal.

A cousin to the typical savings and checking accounts is the money market account. Money market accounts usually pay a higher amount of interest and typically give you checkbook access, but it is important to remember that not all money market accounts are insured by the FDIC and may still be exposed to fluctuations in value. Typically these are not major fluctuations because the people who manage these accounts usually invest in short-term and almost daily transactions. Still, it is always better to have your money insured and protected.

Money market accounts can come with some strings attached. Many require a minimum initial deposit or access limitations in return for a higher interest rate. Some money market accounts provide total checkbook access, while others limit the number of checks per month. Again, the more they limit access, the higher the interest rate you should expect.

We have noticed that a common practice suggested by many financial planners has been to put all your general deposits, such as pension payments or Social Security, directly into your money market account. Then, since the account usually sees higher interest, you can expect your largest cash account to receive the highest amount of interest. But remember that all the interest from banking vehicles is subject to the IRS income tax. No matter what you gain in interest, taxation will reduce it substantially.

Next on the list of bank assets is the certificate of deposit. CDs have sadly become the preferred vehicle of many retired Americans. Retirees on fixed incomes who are wary of the inability of stocks and bonds to create guaranteed income levels will often gravitate towards

CDs. They offer relatively short time periods, and the rates are guaranteed by the contract with the bank. Even though the rate may be 1% or less, retirees are attracted to the guarantees.

Another attractive feature of many CDs is the small penalty associated with early termination. Most CDs will only charge a penalty of half your interest. With current interest rate of 2% or less, that's a very small penalty. It is notable that CD rates have not always been this low. Some of the highest rates were offered back in the 1980s, with rates of 12% or 18% annually. Unfortunately, we are now living with some of the lowest rates, with many hovering around 1%.

As with all banking instruments, it is important to remember that CD interest is taxable each year. If you were lucky enough to earn 4% on your CD this year, your 4% gain is immediately taxable income. Whether you take out the interest or not, that income may affect your tax bracket, Social Security taxation rates, or estate tax calculations. This could be very bad news, especially with our government desperately needing more taxes and with heavy tax increases already underway.

The final assets that are commonly considered to be

within the banking arena are government savings bonds. Savings bonds have no penalty for early withdrawal except for losing the full maturity value. But again, once you liquidate the bond you pay taxes on the interest you received over the course of holding the bond. Savings bonds are also different from CDs in that you don't pay taxes on the interest until you liquidate the bond. Therefore, you can hold the bond for twenty years and not pay interest until you cash it in. But again, as is the case with all banking instruments, the interest is taxable, and usually at the highest tax levels. On the other hand, while savings bonds may not be very practical, they are safe.

It is interesting to note that banking assets are generally not referred to as investments. Instead, they're typically referred to as savings. SEC regulators look at accounts such as CDs, savings accounts, checking accounts, and FDIC-insured money market accounts as savings vehicles, not investments. This is because banking vehicles typically do not expose your money to systematic market risks, and your principal is generally considered safe. Virtually the only risk involved is the opportunity risk of earning only 1% when you could have gained 4% or 5% elsewhere. However, when you add the new litany of bank fees into the equation, some people are beginning to wonder if the banking vehicles actually still provide true capital preservation.

So in summary, the MEGA FG, stable but heavy fuels provide liquidity and availability, but they are highly taxable. They also offer interest rates that are less than inflation rates, so you are actually losing ground over time. If your deposits are protected by FDIC insurance, one might assume that they are safe, but the lengthening list of fees and charges has eroded true capital preservation.

The other option usually offered is the highly volatile Wall Street fuels of stocks, bonds, and mutual funds. But these volatile fuels have been shown to create large systematic losses with unpredictable certainty. If your desired end is a retirement "savings" account, then these types of volatile losses must be avoided. So the question remains: Can a mixture of stable but heavy banking fuels and volatile Wall Street fuels ever get you safely and predictably to an attainable and sustainable retirement?

Chapter 3

A Third Way

Engineers realized early on that mixing RAPTOR X-3 and MEGA FG wouldn't be enough for a successful mission. It might get the colonists to the red planet, if they were lucky, but something more was needed to ensure the survival of the fledgling colony. A simple combination of two conventional options wouldn't work—the mission needed a third option to survive on Mars.

Then mission control hatched a brilliant plan: While the colonists sped off toward their new home, work began on a permanent base on Earth's moon. Raw materials were rocketed out of Earth's atmosphere and deposited at the new lunar depot. There, factories

EVEN WITH A GOOD FUEL MIX, MARS IS A LONG WAY FROM EARTH. RAPTOR X-3 AND MEGA FG ARE NOT ENOUGH—THE MISSION NEEDS A THIRD OPTION.

produced the essential supplies that the colonists would need on Mars. Manufacturing supplies and shipping them to the colony from the moon would use less energy, since the moon's atmosphere and gravity are considerably less than Earth's. In fact, mission control launched the first resupply ships shortly after the colonists left Earth, meaning that a much-needed resupply reached them mere months after they arrived on Mars.

Now supplies could be stockpiled at the lunar depot, and the same ships could be used to make regular shipments to the colonists on Mars. The vessels would then return to Earth, creating a triangular shipping *route. The triangle, long recognized by architects as the strongest of all shapes, became the basis of the third option that the colony needed to sustain its existence.*

Your investments for retirement could benefit from a similar approach. You'll want some money in stocks and bonds and some money in the bank, but that won't be good enough to sustain you during retirement. You need to stockpile your financial pyramid with appropriate amounts of safe investments with adequate

AS THE SHIP SPEEDS TOWARD THE RED PLANET WITH THE COLONISTS AND THEIR SUPPLIES, MISSION CONTROL BUILDS A BASE ON EARTH'S MOON TO SERVE AS A "HALFWAY POINT."

Chapter 3: A Third Way

NOW SUPPLIES CAN BE STOCKPILED AT THE LUNAR DEPOT AND SENT REGULARLY TO THE NEWLY-ESTABLISHED COLONY ON MARS—THE THIRD OPTION THEY NEED.

compound interest that will continually resupply you with life support assets throughout your golden years.

Up until now you've read about how stock brokerage houses and banks have conditioned or trained the American public to balance their money between liquidity, safety, and risk. The banks, we are told, are where you should keep your liquid savings and your safe but small (and always taxable) gains. The stock market is where we are told to put everything else, because without risk there is no reward, and we all know where the most risk is—the stock market! This balancing act between liquidity, safety, and gains has been ingrained into the American public for over thirty years. Rarely does anyone question it, and rarely does anyone even imagine whether there is a better or different way.

Let's review what we have learned so far:

- Liquidity is a real concern. Cash is king, and no sound strategy should neglect short-term needs.

- Consistent and guaranteed gains are desirable for anyone planning on living on a fixed income, including retirees.

- Preserving of your capital and avoiding systematic losses is highly desired and increasingly difficult to maintain in volatile markets such as the ones we now live in.

In this chapter we're going to explore options with you. We will discuss something that Wall Street wishes they could offer: compound interest. Compound interest exists in the banking vehicles because the rates are contractually guaranteed, but it cannot exist in the stock or bond markets due to systematic risk. But unlike the banking industry, we will explore compound interest that is tax-favored and potentially tax-free in some cases. This partially explains why the IRS is not publicizing this information, even though tax law 404 enacts and enables it.

Let's begin by creating what we like to call your Future Proof Scorecard. In the grid's left-hand column we will list all of the features that a Future Proof investor would like their investments or savings to have, plus a few features you don't want. Desirable features include protected capital, liquidity and control, tax-deferred gains, tax-free distributions, compound interest, and tax-free transfer to our heirs. The non-desirable features would be exposure to losses, excessive fees, and contribution limits. Below is a typical example detailing a Future Proof investor's score card.

Feature	What We Want
Protected Capital (no losses)	Yes
Liquidity and Control	Yes
Exposure to Risks and Unpredictable Losses	No
Tax-Deferred Gains	Yes
Tax-Free Distribution	Yes
Contribution Limits	No
Compound Interest Growth	Yes
Excessive Fees	No
Tax-Free Transfer to Heirs	Yes

Let's briefly discuss each one of these features. First is the protection of your capital, or in layman's terms, no more losses! Anyone who had money in the recent Wall Street markets has felt the sting of losses. Case in point is the well-known fact that the decade of 2000-2010 has been deemed the "Lost Decade" because so many retirement stock portfolios will never recover from the losses sustained during that timeframe. Protection and preservation of your capital is a highly desirable feature for any retirement savings account.

The next feature is liquidity and control. Liquidity is a minimum requirement for any financial plan because short-term needs are always present and ignoring them is naïve at best. So liquidity is another desirable feature for any Future Proof investor.

Feature three is exposure to risks and unpredictable losses. This feature is the antithesis to "no more losses," and if feature number one was desirable, then unpredictable losses is obviously undesirable. Yet some may argue that without risks (possible losses) there are no rewards (possible gains). While many will blindly repeat this "risk and rewards" axiom, others disagree. Warren Buffet, for instance, states that his top two laws of investing are "#1 Never lose money" and "#2 See Rule

#1." The same is true for large institutional investing. Institutions such as college endowment funds will move millions of dollars at a time, and their mantra is to participate in upsides (gains), but minimize or eliminate all downsides (losses). So if Warren Buffet and large institutional investors do not follow the risk and reward axiom, then why does Wall Street so actively promote it to the rest of America? Nonetheless, it is obvious that losses of money are never desirable for a retirement funding strategy, so eliminating them as much as possible is just common sense.

The fourth feature is tax-deferred gains. If taxation is deferred, this allows gains to multiply and grow faster. This deferral is a major benefit in most government-qualified plans and a detriment to banking vehicles, where the IRS wants their tax dollars every year.

Feature number five is tax-free distributions. Distribution is that stage in life when you transition from the accumulation phase and begin the income phase and must now live on the withdrawals from the money you have saved. With ordinary income rates averaging 25%-35% on taxable income such as IRA withdrawals, a tax-free income would seem like a 30% bonus in your retirement years. Additionally, tax-free retirement income creates an advantage for any retiree who expects to supplement their retirement incomes with Social Security insurance benefits. This is because the IRS begins taxation of your Social Security benefits after you earn more than $25,000 ($32,000 for couples) in taxable income. But if your primary income is all tax-free, then your Social Security benefits are not taxed. In essense it would be like getting a 30% increase in Social Security benefits. Because of this, tax-free distributions are a highly sought after feature for a Future Proof investor.

The next feature on our Future Proof scorecard is contribution limits. Almost every government-regulated and qualified plan sets limits on how much you can contribute on a yearly basis. These limits are usually tied to your annual income. The more you make, the less they allow you to save. This seems counterintuitive, since high wage earners need to save proportionately more in order to maintain their current lifestyle in retirement. Because of this, any strategy that has contribution limits is counterintuitive and not a desirable feature.

The seventh feature on our scorecard is compound interest. Everyone knows the riddle: "What would you rather have, one million dollars or one penny doubled every day for thirty days?" The obvious decision is to take the million dollars, but the compounding of that penny would create over 2.5 million dollars if you allow compound interest to run its course. Compound interest is also what Albert Einstein is credited as deeming "the most powerful force on earth." Compound interest is the best way to make your money work for you. Compound interest works 24/7/365, and the longer you allow it to occur, the faster your money grows. This is particularly powerful for pre-retirees who can accumulate compound interest for another ten, fifteen, or twenty-five years before drawing income. And as we stated in a previous chapter, if you experience any losses during that accumulation phase, then you have defeated and eliminated your money's ability to compound. This is a very powerful and desirable feature for anyone's retirement savings strategy. In fact, we suggest that this feature is the number one priority for any Future Proof investor with more than ten years of accumulation available before retirement.

The eighth feature is a no brainer. Fees are never a desirable feature. But what constitutes "excessive"? We usually call a fee excessive if it could ultimately deplete your capital. For instance, if you lose money in the stock market and your broker adds insult to injury by still deducting their fees, we call that excessive. This is also true for bank fees that reduce your principal amount faster than the interest they credit to your account. But while this feature is the most obvious, it has also become one of the hardest to monitor and contain. Fee structures have become increasingly more complex as the SEC and other government entities attempt to force the financial institutions to accurately report their fees to their consumers (you and I). Because of this, we always instruct our clients to be diligent in tracking, identifying, and minimizing fees while knowing that absolute freedom from fees is a difficult destination to reach.

Our ninth and final scorecard item is a tax-free transfer to your heirs. While this may not be the least important, it is the final act that you will do with your money. Unfortunately, the IRS learned long ago that the deceased do not have lobbyist and some of the the easiest money to tax is the money you transfer when you pass away. Sometimes referred to as the "death tax," this tax problem can become more headache than blessing for your heirs or favorite charities upon your passing. Therefore, a proper financial strategy inherently includes a plan for transfer to heirs or charities with minimal tax consequences, and a tax-free transfer would be the best result, if it is possible.

Now that we have discussed the features that a Future Proof investor desires and avoids, let's revisit our scorecard, but this time we will populate the top row with the usual financial vehicles.

After completing the Future Proof Scorecard, we quickly realize that what we want might be very different from what we have. It sometimes seems that all the available options come with some level of compromise and that none match all that we want. You might ask yourself, "Is there anything available for the Future Proof investor that includes all the desired features and

Future Proof Scorecard

	What We Want	IRA/401(k)	Roth IRA	Home/Real Estate	Savings/ CDs	Stocks/Bonds/ Mutual Funds	Fixed Annuities
Protected Capital (no losses)	Yes	No	No	No	Yes	No	Yes
Liquidity and Control	Yes	Possible with Loan or Surrender	Possible with Loan or Surrender	Possible with Home Equity Loan	Yes	Yes	Yes, with Possible Penalties
Exposure to Risks and Unpredictable Losses	No	Yes	Yes	Yes	No	Yes	No
Tax-Deferred Gains	Yes	Yes	Yes	Yes	No	Yes	Yes
Tax-Free Distribution	Yes	No	Yes	IRS Limits	No	No	No
Contribution Limits	No	Yes	Yes	No	FDIC Limits	No	No
Compound Interest Growth	Yes	No	No	No	Yes	No	Yes
Excessive Fees	No	Sometimes	Sometimes	No	Sometimes	Sometimes	Sometimes
Tax-Free Transfer to Heirs	Yes	No	No	IRS Limits	No	No	Possible

minimizes or eliminates all the undesirable features?"

Good news! There are options that banks and brokers do not want you to know about. They are not new; in fact, one has been around for as long as the banks and longer than the stock market. Banks have been using one of these options for over a hundred years to grow their wealth without excessive taxation or risk. But they don't want you to know about it because it competes with their savings accounts and CDs. There are literally billions of retirement dollars flowing out of the stock market and into these options every year because they can provide stock-like market gains without exposing your money to stock market risks. As you might imagine, this makes Wall Street very nervous. Brokerage firms and the SEC have tried to squash these options with media propaganda and hype since the late 1990s, but they continue to thrive and grow.

So what is this third option? It is the attainable and sustainable retirement savings balance, a balance of both market-type gains with the safety and liquidity of banking solutions. We will explain these options in detail in later chapters. When they are combined, they create the best retirement savings and income option for most Americans. Let us begin!

CHAPTER 4

SUSTAINING WHAT YOU'VE ATTAINED

Even if the myths aren't true, Mars can be a dangerous place to live.

There were some threats that the colonists were not fully aware of before they arrived on the red planet. For example, it turns out that the plateau where they built their dome is the natural habitat of the Giant Martian Worm (Lumbricus martianus giganticus), a particularly large and dangerous subterranean species. The settlers unwittingly set up shop above a whole nest of the creatures, and vibrations from the colony's power plant upset them terribly. The colony

A NUMBER OF UNKNOWN THREATS COULD MENACE THE MARS COLONY, INCLUDING HOSTILE WILDLIFE LURKING BELOW THE SURFACE.

survived the attack, but repairing the damage was costly.

The colonists were aware of other risks from the very beginning. Meteor showers occasionally pelt the surface of the red planet, posing a threat to the integrity of the dome. The defense force can redirect or destroy meteors before they make impact, but it's almost impossible to predict a meteor shower with any accuracy. This means that settlers have to be vigilant at all times in order to avoid disaster.

Some threats are so unknowable that no one could have predicted or prepared for them. When the colony was invaded by aliens in its third year, the settlers had to think on their feet in order to come out on top. They barely rebuffed the attack thanks to the off-the-cuff ingenuity of the defense force. The Martian colonists learned the hard way that they must be ready for anything.

Investing for retirement is also fraught with risks and pitfalls. There are some threats you may be vaguely aware of but don't think could ever happen to you. Other threats are expected and commonplace, but it's hard to predict when they will strike. Then there are the disasters you never see coming. Tax increases, inflation, stock market crashes, bear markets, recessions, depressions, economic downturns—all of these factors could endanger your hard-earned investments. How will you safeguard your money?

METEOR SHOWERS ARE A KNOWN RISK, BUT THEY ARE DIFFICULT TO PREDICT AND PREPARE FOR.

Chapter 4: Sustaining What You've Attained

NO ONE COULD HAVE PREDICTED THE ALIEN INVASION. COLONISTS ON THE RED PLANET HAVE TO BE READY FOR ANYTHING.

As we mentioned earlier, Albert Einstein, who uncovered the secret of the space-time continuum, is widely credited with the saying, "The most powerful force on earth is the power of compound interest." This is a trustworthy axiom, but we also feel that he should be credited with the saying, "Time is the most powerful force of change and most persistent teacher of knowledge known to man." Mankind has continuously obtained vastly new and different views of reality as time marches on.

Take for instance the retirement planning of the 1950s. Back then the average sixty-five-year-old male was expected to live another 12.8 years. The mortality tables predicted that 50% of retirees would die in their

60s or 70s. At that time, the biggest fear was "dying too soon."

Now fast forward to the Baby Boomers and compare their retirement planning to their parent's. Boomers are being told that the new America will have 25% of the population over the age of sixty-five, twenty million people will live beyond age eighty-five, and another one million will live past the age of one hundred. Today's retirement planning fear has changed from dying too soon to living too long and outliving your money!

Furthermore, there are twelve major risks to your retirement, and we think you can guess what number one is:

12. Entitlement risk: The risk that government programs like Medicare, Social Security, and others will not provide income sufficient for your retirement.

11. Excess withdrawal risk: The risk of draining your savings too quickly.

10. Lifestyle risk: The risk that your income during retirement will not be enough to maintain your current or projected standard of living.

9. Asset allocation risk: The risk of failing to adequately

diversify your assets by being either too conservative or too aggressive.

8.   Inflation risk: The risk that rising costs due to inflation will undermine the purchasing power of your retirement investments.

7.   Medical expense risk: The risk of paying for the growing cost of healthcare-related services in retirement.

6.   Tax risk: The risk that rising or unforeseen taxes will wreak havoc on your portfolio or purchasing power.

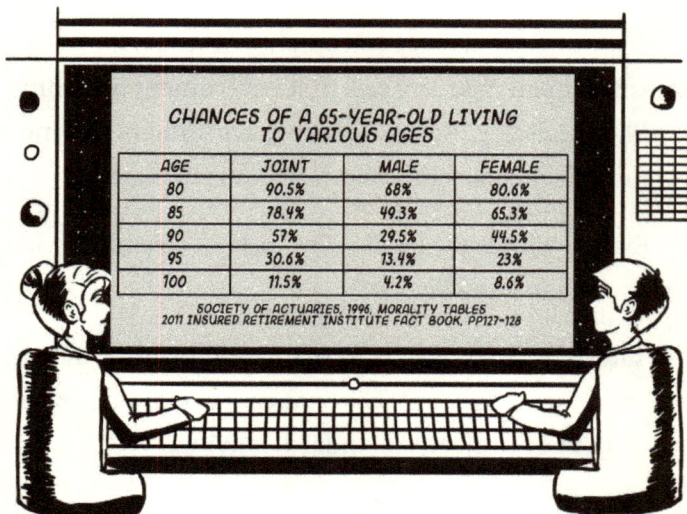

CHANCES OF A 65-YEAR-OLD LIVING TO VARIOUS AGES

AGE	JOINT	MALE	FEMALE
80	90.5%	68%	80.6%
85	78.4%	49.3%	65.3%
90	57%	29.5%	44.5%
95	30.6%	13.4%	23%
100	11.5%	4.2%	8.6%

SOCIETY OF ACTUARIES, 1996, MORALITY TABLES
2011 INSURED RETIREMENT INSTITUTE FACT BOOK, PP127-128

5. Personal or event risk: The risk that unexpected changes in family circumstances will undermine your retirement plans (includes spousal survivor risk).

4. Market risk: The risk of losing retirement assets temporarily or permanently due to market downturn or poor investment performance.

3. Incapacity risk: The risk that as a result of deteriorating health, you may no longer be able to manage your financial affairs.

2. Sequence of returns risk: The risk of receiving low or negative returns in the early years and diminishing your retirement portfolio.

1. Longevity risk: The risk of outliving your retirement assets.

It's time to admit that retirement has never been an age or a birthday present. It has always been a financial decision. Reaching and then maintaining retirement is a financial endeavor. In the 1950s our parents were taught to work for thirty years at the same company, draw a pension, and then augment that with government programs like Social Security. But again, time has changed all that. The guaranteed annual pension check income has been replaced with IRAs and 401(k)s. Social Security is no longer a given either, as it suffers from years of political fiduciary abuse and the simple mathematics of a decreasing number of producers and an increasing number of recipients.

Consequently, the new retirement needed a new mathematical model. Enter the balanced portfolio and the 4% drawdown rule. In 1994, in response to the increasing need for a new model, William Bengen wrote a thesis regarding safe retirement withdrawal rates titled "Determining Withdrawal Rates Using Historical Data." Bengen's research attempted to reveal what a safe annual retirement withdrawal percentage should (theoretically) be when adjusted for inflation. This prominent thesis determined that 4% of a portfolio's value (comprised of a "balanced portfolio" of 50% stocks and 50% bonds) could be safely withdrawn from the initial portfolio and then annually adjusted for inflation for forty years. The thesis answered the nagging questions that many clients were asking, and the world of financial planning accepted the thesis as fact and even named it the 4% balanced portfolio rule. For the next twenty years, all financial plans were built around the 4% rule. But remember what we stated earlier about time. It is a powerful force, and if your financial plan is currently built on the basis of the 4% rule, we suggest you pay close attention.

Wall Street's wholesale adoption of Bengen's thesis was predictable because it masked a multitude of sins. For one, the proposed portfolio was 100% stocks and bonds. This assumes no other mix is required or acceptable, and that naturally pleased Wall Street. The other was that in 1994 it used the unprecedented bull run of the 1980s and early 1990s stock market for its underlying assumptions. This created the illusion of a constantly rising and somewhat safe stock market, as if systematic risk was something you could just wait out. This legitimized the axioms of long-term investing and the buy and hold strategy. For nearly twenty years this was regarded as the only acceptable retirement strategy, and anything else was deemed ludicrous or unsound.

Unfortunately for Wall Street and millions of Baby Boomers, time marches on and exposes all. By 2008, the stock market losses of 2001 and 2007 caused many of the mathematical models using the 4% rule to fail. That year, Nobel laureate William Sharpe published a paper stating that the 4% rule had a failure rate of 10-15%. The "rule" now had exceptions and might be in need of a new name!

Chapter 4: Sustaining What You've Attained

Further mathematical erosion occurs when you fast-forward to our recent historical long run of low interest rates, combined with the fact that Bengen's work was only based upon the stock, bond, and inflation history of the American twentieth century, not the twenty-first century that we will be retiring in. Thus, it's not surprising that in 2013, Wade Pfau wrote a research paper entitled "An International Perspective on Safe Withdrawal Rates: The Demise of the 4 Percent Rule?" In it, Pfau states that the U.S. markets of the twentieth century were prosperous when compared to the other major developed countries, and using just twentieth-century American market data to project future stock market returns would lead to "success bias" and "irrational optimism." Unfortunately for the seventy-six million U.S. Baby Boomers now heading into retirement, many economists now believe that the U.S. economy of the twenty-first century will more likely resemble that of Europe in the twentieth century rather than the U.S. markets of the same period.

Pfau's paper also exposed an inherent risk of the 4% rule in today's volatile markets. Pfau named this risk "equity sequence of returns." It refers to the fact that the timing of your 4% withdrawals must coincide with up markets for the rule to work consistently. If your withdrawals begin during a down market, the so-called rule will fail. Alas, systematic risk raises its ugly head again, as no one can accurately predict which way or at what time the market will go up or down. Therefore, the 4% rule cannot determine when or how much you should withdraw.

As if this wasn't enough bad news, Pfau went on to co-author another paper titled "The 4% Rule Is Not Safe in a Low-Yield World." This paper evaluated the Bengen assumption of a 50% bond portfolio in our unusually low-yield bond market that is 4% lower than the historical norm. Again, an inherent risk in a volatile market is sequence of returns, and this is no different in the bond markets. The essay called this risk "bond-yield sequence of returns" and concluded that a current retiree with a 50/50 stocks and bonds portfolio who withdraws an inflation-adjusted 4% would have a 57% chance of portfolio failure. Portfolio failure was defined as the retirement account running out of money entirely.

Time marches on, but while millions of Americans still follow this advice and have their entire retirement strategy built on a 4% rule that only succeeds 43% of the time, Wall Street conveniently ignores the facts. Why,

Risk of Equity Sequence of Returns: Losses at Beginning of Period

Year	Beginning Amount	Hypothetical Return	Balance After Annual Withdrawal $4,000 + 3% Inflation
1	$100,000	-18%	$78,120
2	$78,120	-21%	$57,595
3	$57,595	8%	$57,959
4	$57,595	-5%	$50,690
5	$50,690	13%	$52,778
6	$52,778	-15%	$40,224
7	$40,224	5%	$37,459
8	$37,459	-17%	$26,171
9	$26,171	15%	$25,030
10	$25,030	8%	$21,813
11	$21,813	22%	$21,237
12	$21,237	4%	$16,549
13	$16,549	-12%	$8,860
14	$8,860	11%	$3,961
15	$3,961	8%	$-
16	$-	-12%	$-
17	$-	18%	$-
18	$-	16%	$-
19	$-	6%	$-
20	$-	15%	$-

you ask? As they said in the Watergate movie, "follow the money." Wall Street hasn't come up with a better way to keep your money in their hands, so they are opportunely quiet while they search for another "they-win-you-lose" alternative.

So what alternative is there to the 4% rule and its

Risk of Equity Sequence of Returns: Reversing the Losses

Year	Beginning Amount	Hypothetical Return	Balance After Annual Withdrawal $4,000 + 3% Inflation
1	$100,000	15%	$111,120
2	$111,120	6%	$113,667
3	$113,667	16%	$127,610
4	$127,610	18%	$146,209
5	$146,209	-12%	$124,162
6	$124,162	8%	$129,458
7	$129,458	11%	$138,922
8	$138,922	-12%	$117,332
9	$117,332	4%	$116,958
10	$116,958	22%	$137,470
11	$137,470	8%	$143,092
12	$143,092	15%	$159,019
13	$159,019	-17%	$126,283
14	$126,283	5%	$126,723
15	$126,723	-15%	$101,664
16	$101,664	13%	$108,648
17	$108,648	-5%	$96,797
18	$96,797	8%	$97,929
19	$97,929	-21%	$70,554
20	$70,554	-18%	$50,841

failures? Since the name of this book is Future Proof Investing, one might expect a new and previously unheard of concept with a big name and an unproved thesis to replace the old one. And while time changes many things, it also produces time-tested solutions, and Future Proofing has more to do with lessons learned than it does with speculation.

Rewind back to the 1950s, before the current IRA and 401(k) retirement strategies that we have been trained to rely on. Our parents' retirement strategy involved constant contribution into a pension that on retirement day began annual income payments that lasted for thirty years or more. If you died early, your pension annuity payments continued on to your heirs until depleted. Social Security was also based on years of consistent contribution, and at retirement it triggered annual, annuitized payments for the rest of your life. Similar to pension payments, if you died early, your Social Security payments were available to your heirs. So the fear of dying early was mitigated.

Now fast forward to today's Baby Boomer and apply the 1950s pension strategy to our new fear of living too long and outliving our money. Let's see if the old and discredited concept of a pension and annuitized payment stream will work here. We would consistently contribute to a plan exactly the same way we are instructed to contribute to IRAs and 401(k)s, but instead of betting on the stock market, we build a fund that can trigger annual and predictable retirement payments for the next thirty years or even the rest of our life, no matter how long we live. Add a feature similar to the Social Security cost-of-living increase to make our lifetime annual pension payments keep up with inflation, and we have created an answer to our greatest fear of outliving our money while mitigating the risk of inflation.

This seems to be a time-tested solution—so why is it not being employed anymore? The first reason is encapsulated in the phrase, "follow the money." The time-tested pension strategy does not put money into the stock market or the IRS's tax coffers. It does not put money into bank deposits. Therefore, it cannot be acceptable to the marketing firms being paid by these institutions. Couple this with Baby Boomers' inherent affinity for maintaining control at all times and the finality of the decision to choose predetermined annuitized payments with the implied loss of control, and you will see how Wall Street marketing has been able to foster a general aversion to this time-tested strategy. The irony of this is how much retirees love Social Security and pensions, yet shun anything called an annuity payment. All three are, in fact, virtually the same creature packaged differently. We refer to it as the "retirement pension puzzle."

Now that you understand the basis behind the irony and the puzzle, let's progress beyond the marketing hype and take a fresh look at the problem. Will you outlive your money? Is your retirement sustainable using your current plan? Would a fresh look at time-tested principals be advantageous? Let's begin again.

We stated previously that Future Proofing your retirement starts by answering four simple questions. These questions comprise the entire speculative realm of a Future Proofed retirement. They are:

1. Do you believe that in the future taxes will be higher or lower?

2. What is the inflation-adjusted retirement income level that you desire?

3. Will you outlive your money during retirement?

4. What do you wish for your heirs after you pass away?

The first two questions frame the answer for the third question, and the fourth question is one that many Baby Boomers have not yet put much thought into. Based on history, the third phase of retirement planning is wealth transfer planning, and most retirees don't prepare for this phase until it is too late. In the following paragraphs we will discuss income planning that incorporates these four questions, followed by an analysis of an updated version of your parents pension-type income planning that was designed specifically for Boomers who want more control.

1. Do you believe that in the future taxes will be higher or lower?

Too many times we assume that we know how people will answer this question. While it seems obvious to us that taxes always go up, about two out of every ten people we ask will answer with "I don't know" or "lower." As a result, we have stopped asking until after we have guided the person through an investigation of the history of taxes in America.

Since 1900 there have consistently been spikes in the IRS tax rates in years that coincided with major military conflicts such as WWI, WWII, Korea, and Vietnam. Surprisingly, the recent wars in Iraq and Afghanistan have yet to trigger the tax increase. This partially explains the skyrocketing national debt of the past decade.

In addition, the federal government has created entitlement programs such as Medicare, Medicaid, Social Security, and most recently a national health care program. All of these programs can stay funded as long as the majority of users are young and healthy. If more and more users begin to fail in health, or reach the age where they trigger payments instead of contributing, the systems will collapse without an infusion of tax dollars to bail them out.

Now consider the pending Boomers' retirements. That's right, pending. The largest influx of retirees and aging Americans has yet to retire. Over the next ten to fifteen years their numbers will steadily grow to a proportion that this country or any country has never experienced. The stress and strain on entitlement programs will increase exponentially every year for the next fifteen to twenty-five years. The only solutions will be more tax dollars from fewer contributors or ending the entitlement programs. If you believe our politicians will end them and risk being voted out of office, think again.

We could go further: bailouts, pork-barrel projects, wars and rumors of wars—the list never stops. This and many other insights we have uncovered over the years are why we instinctively answer that taxes are going to go up. In our humble opinion, they are going to go up a lot.

So why do we care about taxation when we are

planning our retirement income? The first reason is that the IRS suggests we employ what they call tax-deferred IRAs and 401(k)s. Tax-deferred means you don't pay taxes while your money accumulates; you pay taxes when you begin making withdrawals. Assume you deferred taxes back when the top tax rate was 25%. Then when you take the money out the tax rate is 35%. This is good for the IRS because any tax savings you thought you had are essentially wiped out, but worst of all is that your cash flow income level is reduced by 35% before you ever get to spend it.

We can guess what you're about to say: "I am going to live on two thirds of my income at retirement, and taxes will be lower for me." We wouldn't bet on that. First of all, you would still be losing 35% of your money right off the top. So if you are planning your retirement with IRAs and 401(k)s, join one of our workshops, use the calculators to see if your taxation rates might kill your retirement plan, and explore tax free options.

2. What is the inflation-adjusted retirement income level that you desire?

Inflation is compound interest in reverse. A widely accepted inflation rate is 3% annually, and our federal government does lots of interesting math to create the illusion that this is what we are still experiencing—but that is a topic for another time. Today, let's simply use the 3% number and have some fun on your calculator. Take your current income amount and subtract 30%. This is the proverbial two thirds of your income that financial planners say is a good goal. Now hit the following key sequence twenty times: <+> <3> <%>. The resultant number is your inflation-adjusted two thirds of your income if retirement was twenty years out. It's always amazing how 3% can grow quickly if given enough time, and inflation is another retirement income killer that should never be ignored!

Now look at your current retirement income planning. Does it have inflation adjustments like we calculated above? More importantly, does it automatically adjust your income levels up with inflation? Unfortunately, too many retirement plans have ignored or are not able to include either of these. Future Proof retirement planning includes both.

3. Will you outlive your money during retirement?

This is actually the real question that we all want answered.

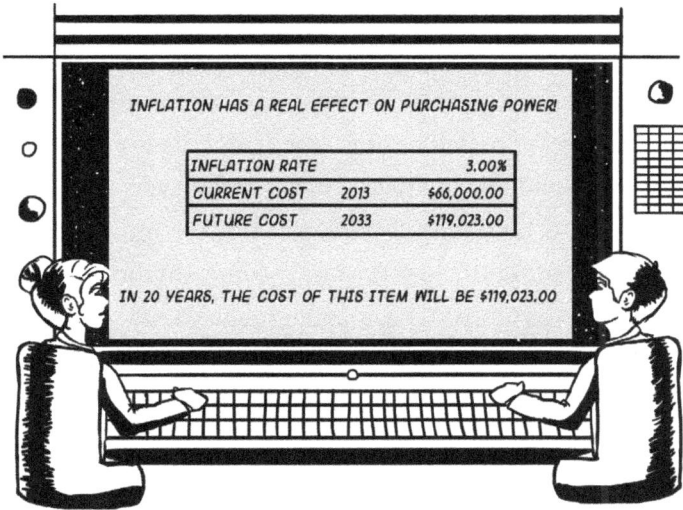

INFLATION HAS A REAL EFFECT ON PURCHASING POWER!

INFLATION RATE		3.00%
CURRENT COST	2013	$66,000.00
FUTURE COST	2033	$119,023.00

IN 20 YEARS, THE COST OF THIS ITEM WILL BE $119,023.00

In question one we estimated which way you believe taxes will go during your retirement. In Future Proof income planning we use a current tax table and apply an acceptable adjustment, based on our question number one discussion, to each income range. We then use that new table as our predicted tax table at time of retirement.

Next, we record the inflation-adjusted income level that we desire from step number two. Then we find that income level on the predicted tax table at time of retirement and subtract that percentage from the income number. This will be your net retirement income cash flow. That's all you will have to live on in retirement. If this is acceptable, then your inflation-adjusted income level is adequate and can be used for step three. If it is too low, then you must increase the inflation-adjusted income level and do the same steps until the net number is acceptable. This step gets very easy when you are using tax-free and tax-favored incomes, but for most of you who are reading this book, your income streams are set up to be taxed at ordinary income rates when you retire.

In step three you simply multiply your inflation-adjusted income level by thirty and record the value. This is the dollar amount you would need at the time of retirement to last thirty years, assuming no inflation and that your funds experienced no gains, or more importantly, no losses during retirement.

Now comes the fun part. We know that inflation is generally quoted at 3% per year, so we must strive to gain at least that much per year in compound interest to offset inflation. How can you do that? Stock market gains and losses are not compound interest. We also know that the stock market of the twenty-first century will be vastly different from the stock market of the twentieth century. Experts predict an elevator-type stock market, not an escalator. The elevator will be going up and down like a piston, and no one can predict when, in which direction, or how high or low it will go each time. This is the main reason that the old 4% rule is now failing 57% of the time.

We also realize that bank CDs and bank deposits are no longer paying anywhere close to the 3% interest we need to keep up with inflation. And even if they did, that interest would be offset by IRS taxation, leaving a need of even higher than 3% interest to keep up. We don't think that will happen anytime soon, though we can hope. However, "hope is not a strategy." Thus, the typical conclusion is that inflation concerns and elevator movement stock markets render the stock market and/or bank products unacceptable and unreliable retirement income vehicles.

Conversely, a properly established Future Proof Plan (FPP) does gain a guaranteed compound interest rate that is generally higher than inflation. If a portion of your retirement funding was already in an FPP at your time of retirement, that portion would keep up or exceed inflation. Also, FPPs do not follow the stock market roller coaster. They gain annual interest, so the 4% rule risk of timing is also eliminated. Proper use of your FPP creates a tax-free income stream and eliminates the 35% tax loss every year. It also reduces the annual amount needed and helps your nest egg to last longer, no matter how high taxes go up.

Now you are beginning to see what Future Proofing actually means. Tax-free eliminates the uncertainty of future IRS tax hikes and penalties, and in a moment we will do some real world examples showing the gains you can achieve for your retirement income versus an IRA or 401(k). As for Boomers wanting more control, an FPP for retirement funding allows you to maintain 100% control.

Later on in this chapter we will dissect some charts that illustrate the numbers behind Future Proof retirement income planning versus the old 4% rule retirement income planning, but in summary, an FPP can positively answer the "Will I outlive my money?" question. Even better, unlike the pension plans of our parents, FPPs still leave the retiring Boomer with full financial control. Pension payments with growth, safety, and control—that is the Future Proof retirement income planning goal.

4. What do you wish for your heirs after you pass away?

This question is one that every parent thinks

about, but in all the retirement uncertainty that we are currently facing, self-preservation looms so large that we force this issue to the "to-do-maybe" list in our retirement planning. And let's face it: if you use a 50/50 stock and bond portfolio and a 4% drawn down, you are planning to be near penniless at time of death. That is the way it is designed; transfer of whatever is left over is an insignificant issue.

But imagine for a moment liquidity and growth while you accumulate, followed by predictable income while you are retired, and then a nearly worry-free and tax-free wealth transfer vehicle to provide an inheritance for your heirs. That is indeed Future Proof investing for your retirement.

Future Proof retirement planning inherently includes the mechanism to transfer wealth to your children when you pass away. No additional planning is needed. Just save for your retirement and then retire with less risk, and the wealth transfer upon your passing is already taken care of. Try and do that with a balanced stock portfolio or laddered CDs—it just doesn't happen anywhere else.

Now that you have answered the four questions for

yourself and have an understanding of what a Future Proof retirement plan can provide, we said we would provide some charts for those of you who want more empirical proofs. So if you are a numbers person, take a look below. But if you are ready to move forward, then simply turn to the next chapter and we will get one step closer to planning your Future Proof investing and retirement.

Investable Assets: $500,000
Hypothetical & Typical Asset Allocation:

	Banks/CDs	Future Proof Plan	Stocks/ Bonds	
Current %	10%	0%	90%	
2000-2009 S&P 500 Returns:	3% $50,000	7% $0	S&P 500 $450,000	Total $500,000
-10.14%	$51,500	$0	$404,370	$455,870
-13.04%	$53,045	$0	$351,640	$404,685
-23.37%	$54,636	$0	$269,462	$324,098
26.38	$56,275	$0	$340,546	$396,821
8.99%	$57,964	$0	$371,161	$429,125
3.00%	$59,703	$0	$382,296	$441,998
13.62%	$61,494	$0	$434,464	$495,858
3.53%	$63,339	$0	$449,698	$513,036
-38.49%	$65,239	$0	$276,609	$341,848
19.67%	$67,196	$0	$331,018	$398,214
Total After 10 Years	$67,196	$0	$331,018	$398,214

Assumes a typical allocation of 90% stocks and 10% bank CDs. A
$500,000 initial balance results in losses, reducing the total down to
$398,214 during the "Lost Decade."

Current Asset Allocation:
Hypothetical & Typical Future Proof Asset Allocation

	Banks/CDs	Future Proof Plan	Stocks/ Bonds	
Current %	10%	60%	30%	
2000-2009 S&P 500 Returns:	3% $50,000	7% $300,000	S&P 500 $150,000	Total $500,000
-10.14%	$51,500	$300,000	$134,790	$486,290
-13.04%	$53,045	$300,000	$117,213	$470,258
-23.37%	$54,636	$300,000	$89,821	$444,457
26.38	$56,275	$321,000	$113,515	$490,791
8.99%	$57,964	$343,470	$123,720	$525,154
3.00%	$59,703	$353,774	$127,432	$540,909
13.62%	$61,494	$378,538	$144,788	$584,820
3.53%	$63,339	$391,901	$149,899	$605,138
-38.49%	$65,239	$391,901	$92,203	$549,342
19.67%	$67,196	$419,334	$110,339	$596,869
Total After 10 Years	$67,196	$419,334	$110,339	$596,869

A Future Proof suggested allocation of 60% Future Proof with a maximum of 30% in stocks and 10% in bank CDs. A $500,000 initial balance grows to $596,869 during the "Lost Decade."

CHAPTER 5

YOUR LIFE SUPPORT ASSETS

What's the difference between a colony and a base? And which one would you want to build on Mars?

Early mission plans proposed that a base would be the best option for humanity's first attempt at living on the red planet. A bare-bones structure, it would be easy and inexpensive to build. But with little more than living quarters and docking bays, the Mars base could never become self-sufficient. Colonists would have to rely on shipments of supplies coming from the lunar depot, and if a supply shipment was ever late or could not be sent for some reason, they would be in big trouble. Mankind could survive on the red planet, but they would never be able to thrive.

Chapter 5: Your Life Support Assets

Mission control soon abandoned this idea in favor of constructing a fully-functioning Mars colony. They supplemented their original blueprints with farms, orchards, hydroponics laboratories, and factories. The colonists' ship was stocked with a variety of life support assets, including seeds and live plants that could be cultivated when they reached their new home. They even brought farm animals to raise for protein. Unlike a base, this colony would quickly become independent

EARLY MISSION PLANS PROPOSED SIMPLY BUILDING A BASE ON THE RED PLANET. BUT IT WOULD ALWAYS NEED TO BE RESUPPLIED FROM THE LUNAR DEPOT AND COULD NEVER BE INDEPENDENT.

INSTEAD, MISSION CONTROL OPTED FOR A SELF-SUFFICIENT COLONY. AFTER ITS INITIAL PHASE, IT COULD PRODUCE ALL THE FOOD AND SUPPLIES IT WOULD EVER NEED.

of Earth, so an interruption in shipping would present no real danger. Colonists would grow their own food, breathe air produced by their own trees, and manufacture any and all goods they could ever need.

A colony is superior to a base in one more important way: Because of its prosperity and self-sufficiency, the Mars colony will eventually be able to launch colonies of its own. The settlers' effective planning will benefit not only themselves, but also their children and children's children on faraway worlds.

When it comes to your retirement, are you building a base or a colony? Are you putting up as many assets

UNLIKE A BASE, A COLONY CAN LAUNCH OTHER COLONIES, PASSING ON ITS PROSPERITY TO THE NEXT GENERATIONS ON OTHER PLANETS.

as you can, perhaps without the benefit of compound interest, and hoping that the money won't run out before you die? When your income dries up, will your finances be self-sufficient and sustainable? If the markets crashed, would your finances crash too? More importantly, will there be anything left over for your family when you pass? When you Future Proof your investments, you ensure that not only will you be taken care of in your retirement, your children and grandchildren will share in your legacy.

Have you ever heard the phrase, "money is the root of all evil"? Most people have, but very few know that it is a misquotation of the original verse. The actual verse reads, "the love of money is the root of all evil." Those three words create a completely different statement and greater understanding for the reader.

The word "annuity" has experienced a similar misfortune. An annuity is defined as any continuing payment with a fixed total annual amount. The root word is "annual," and the "-ity" ending indicates an action, in this case payments. So an annuity is an annual payment stream. Knowing this, should it surprise us when you hear a stock broker or banker (or TV talking head) tell horror stories about annuities? Those evil annual payments? Annuity advice from these talking heads reminds us of the Chevy dealer who tells you all the bad things about the new Fords. Not once will he describe a specific Ford model, just broad generalizations. It is a simple case of a competitor spewing all the fear, uncertainty, and doubt he can about his competitor.

Thus, the fact that many people have heard or said many negative things in the media about annuities and that there could be some drawbacks to owning any annuity is not surprising. In fact, in the next few paragraphs we will describe the pros and cons of this asset class. Some may be more suited to an individual's needs then others, but if you were to believe the competitors at the banks and brokers, you would be led to believe that this whole class of assets should never be used because of a bad experience of one person they know of or have heard about. But brokers hope that we will never apply this same logic to the stock market. If we did, simply because of a few bad apples or the 2008 crash, for instance, nobody should ever buy mutual funds, municipal bonds, or stocks. Would your broker tell you to stop buying stocks because many of the mutual funds lost 48% in 2008 and retirees lost a decade of gains almost overnight? Would they tell you to stop buying bonds because of the Enron debacle? Maybe you should stop buying them, but maybe not—it all depends on one's financial needs and whether these instruments fit the bill.

An annuity is a contract with an insurance company similar to the way that a CD is a contract with a bank. Other similarities between CDs and annuities are:

- CDs and annuities both require a time commitment. You must leave the money in place for a pre-described amount of time.

- The longer the time you leave it there, the greater the interest you earn.

- If you completely withdraw all the money before the

agreed upon time commitment, you will be penalized with a surrender charge.

The differences between an average CD and an annuity is that annuities are expected to pay 300% more for the same or similar time requirement. But the surrender charges for not completing the time commitment in an annuity are much higher than the bank CDs. Another way that annuities are different than CDs is that annuities offer choices for how to liquidate the asset if you were to die during the time commitment period—hence the insurance portion. The last difference is that unlike CDs, annuities are designed to create income streams after the time commitment is up. This is one reason why annuities are so popular for retirement.

In fact, prior to the 1980s, all pensions were essentially annuity contracts. A pension is a defined benefit contract. The benefit is defined for the retiree as previously defined annual payments during retirement. Contrast that to the 401(k)s and IRAs that replaced the pension. These IRS-qualified plans are defined contribution plans, not defined benefit. Your contributions can be defined, but your benefits during retirement are no longer guaranteed or known.

Chapter 5: Your Life Support Assets

While all annuities are designed to create annual payment streams after a predetermined time commitment (the accumulation period), there are different versions designed for different needs. These versions can be divided into four subcategories:

1. Single pay immediate annuity (SPIA)

2. Fixed deferred annuity (fixed)

3. Variable deferred annuity (variable)

4. Fixed indexed annuity (FIA)

The SPIA is unique because it begins annual payments immediately after the policy is funded. All the others are deferred annuity types, meaning that the payment streams start in the future after the accumulation period reaches its term. SPIAs are usually used for short-term, high annual payment streams after a lump sum of money has been deposited into the policy.

The SPIA can have a major drawback: many SPIA contracts have a life-only annuity payment schedule. So when you die, your life is over, and so are the life-only payments. The pro of the SPIA is that the annual payments are higher relative to other annuity types, and this sometimes entices retirees who are so used to taking risks. Unfortunately, when they pass away, their heirs blame the evil annuity and tell horror stories about how the insurance company kept their inheritance when grandpa died. SPIAs do have a place, but these are definitely not what we call retirement-ready annuities.

While some argue that there are many more than three types of deferred annuities, all recognize the fact that there are two major categories: fixed and variable. These two are very different. The differences are primarily in the accumulation period and what happens to your premiums during that time. But even though they are vastly different, one thing remains the same: they are both contracts with an insurance company for predefined annuity payments in the future.

First we will cover the variable annuity, or as we call it, the "evil twin." Variable annuities were invented back in the 1980s and 90s to compete with the stock market. When you purchase a variable annuity, your premiums go into a fund at the insurance company. You get many fund options to choose from, and these are referred to as side accounts. Side accounts act similarly to mutual funds. They are not technically mutual funds, but they are managed by some of the same managers and offer some of the same results. Variable annuities are the only annuities that expose your premium to the systematic risks of the stock market. If you are familiar with stock purchases, then variable annuities will be very familiar. You may see names like American Funds, T. Rowe Price, Janus, Fidelity, and others. You also get the standard "balanced portfolio" advice as you choose from a range of fund strategies such as growth, value, or emerging markets.

Another similarity to mutual funds is the fact that variable annuities charge management fees. Typical variable annuity expenses can range anywhere from 1-5%, depending on the options you choose. Other fees that variable annuities have are mortality and expense. These could be anywhere from 1 to 1.5%, and they pay for the death benefit and general expenses inside the annuity. It's different from stock market vehicles in that the issuing insurance company provides an enhanced death benefit that guarantees not only your deposit but increases your benefit to your heirs if you pass away. In short, variable annuities can have very complicated and sometimes very large fee structures.

Variable annuities were very popular during the market rise of the 80s and 90s because they offered many features that you just couldn't get inside a typical stock market vehicle. But because of the fee structure and the fact that your premiums are exposed directly to the systematic risk of the stock market, variable annuities are only sold by brokerage houses and brokers that are SEC-licensed. Today, many financial planners, including us, question the continued validity of variable annuities within retirement savings plans. But like every financial vehicle, there is still a place for them, but today that place is much smaller, and we do not consider variable annuities to be retirement-ready annuities.

Now let's talk about fixed annuities and then fixed indexed annuities. Unlike variable annuities, the main characteristic of fixed annuities is protection of your principal. Your premium dollars are never exposed to systematic market risks, and the premium amounts credited to your account can only grow or stay the same. They will never go down until you make a withdrawal. So how does a fixed annuity provide growth during the accumulation period? Unlike variable annuities, fixed annuities credit a predetermined interest payment to your account on a periodic basis, and the interest grows in a compounded manner. The issuing insurance company in a traditional fixed annuity will announce the interest rate that it will credit for the year in advance, much like a bank announces its interest rates on CDs. The main difference is that fixed annuities currently pay 364% higher interest rates than bank CDs.[1]

Another interesting difference from CDs is the fact that your gains are tax-deferred. Therefore, unlike CDs, the annuity interest grows without a tax drag. Fixed annuities' tax advantages continue during the annuity payment period as well, since annuity payments are considered tax-favored, unlike any other payment stream.

Fixed annuities are sometimes considered retirement-ready annuities. Though we feel that fixed annuities are an excellent alternative to CDs, and a great option for those who need an alternative to the systematic risks that have plagued their retirement savings, we feel that another step is better. That step is the fixed annuity's big brother, the fixed indexed annuity (FIA).

Fixed annuities and fixed indexed annuities have many similarities. They both provide protection of principal, which means no matter how much the stock market loses, you will not. This satisfies Warren Buffet's

1   Annuity interest rate for November 2013: 2.875% per the Federal Retirement Thrift Investment Board's annuity rate index.

rules: "#1: Never lose money. #2: See rule #1." Both have the option of guaranteed payments for the remainder of your life, and unlike the life only annuity we described previously, they both have death benefit options that transfer your wealth to your heirs (tax-free in most cases) when you die. Both grow tax-deferred, so you can experience true compound interest gains in your wealth, and both offer tax-favored payments during the annuity payment.

While both credit your account balance with periodic interest payments, here is where the difference begins. The difference that separates a traditional fixed annuity from fixed indexed annuities is interest crediting methods. Fixed annuities credit a predetermined and consistent interest amount each year. While this is growing wealth on a consistent basis, many pre-retirees deem this to be too slow. The subtle contrast in a FIA is how the amount of interest to credit is determined. The FIA's interest rate is proportional to an index performance. The index performance used could be the Dow Jones or the S&P 500 index, for example. Thus, if the index goes up by 5%, the annuity might pay 5%. If the index rose by 10%, the annuity might pay 10%. This is the basic mechanism for the proportional interest gains within an FIA. An important feature of an FIA is that once that interest is credited to the account, those credits are permanently retained in the account and become part of the protected principal. Conversely, if the chosen index goes down, the principal and previous years' gains are protected, but the owner of the FIA would receive zero interest and no loss of principal. Thus, FIAs participate in the upsides but never the downturns.

Here's a simple and typical example of the way an FIA can work for you. Let's say you put $100,000 into a typical FIA that uses the S&P 500's performance as the index performance benchmark. Now imagine that at the end of the first year the S&P 500 index went up by 10%. Your FIA would be eligible to receive a 10% interest payment that year. Assuming your contract paid 100% proportional to the index performance, then the interest paid would be 10% ($10,000), and that would now become part of your new protected principal (now $110,000). This new protected principal amount adjustment is sometimes referred to as an annual reset.

Now imagine that the next year the index went down by 30%. Your FIA started the year at $110,000, but the index went negative. An FIA typically has a minimum interest rate guaranteed to never go lower than 0%

(called a floor), and we will assume that as well for this example. Thus, you would receive 0% interest that year and still have $110,000 in your account. We know many Americans who would have loved to have had this result back in 2007 or 2008.

This concept of a financial growth vehicle that never goes down and only goes up or stays flat is very hard for most people to believe or comprehend. But in its simplest form, if the stock market index goes down, you don't lose any money. If it goes up, you participate in the gains! This is the main reason why we recommend FIAs as the choice for a retirement-ready annuity.

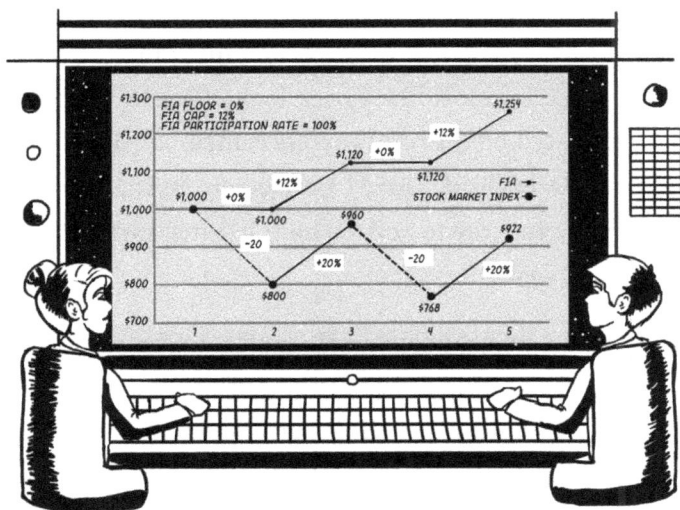

FIAs provide growth and safety in one easily managed financial vehicle.

It is important to note that unlike a variable annuity, FIA premium account values are not invested in the stock market or exposed to systematic risks. FIAs are a contract with the insurance company, and the interest paid is periodic and variable dependent on the fluctuations of a given index. That index could be a stock market index or otherwise.

Also note that the issuing insurance company guarantees all fixed annuities, including FIAs, similar to the way CDs are guaranteed by the banks. You might say that the FDIC can back bank CDs, and you're right, up to some arbitrary value. But again, it is insurance on your deposit that has most likely been loaned out by the bank to a calculated credit risk (anyone remember the Home Mortgage Debacle of 2008?). Conversely, fixed annuities are already insurance and include life insurance death benefits as well.

Initially, some people will say that FIAs look too good to be true. While they are vastly better than the alternatives offered by banks and stockbrokers, they too have their downsides. The first is the depth of terms that you must understand to evaluate which FIA fits best for you. Below we will attempt to simplify these for the average reader. Bear in mind that this is not an exhaustive dissertation, but simply a primer. You should seek qualified assistance before selecting an FIA for your retirement needs.

FIA terms are divided into income options (terms for how payments can be received) and accumulation period terms. What you need to know about FIA accumulation options and terms can be summarized in these three areas, and beware: this section can become very dry and mathematically boring.

Floor and Ceiling Interest Rates

The floor interest rate is the minimum interest rate that your account will receive should the index value go negative for that crediting period. No FIA should ever have a floor less than 0%. Today, many FIAs are offering a floor interest rate of 1% or 2% in exchange for concessions on other terms, but the usual and expected floor is 0%. The ceiling is sometimes referred to as the cap amount and is the maximum interest percentage that the policy will pay no matter how high the index climbs. For instance, if you had a cap of 10% and the index went up by 15% that period, then your account would not receive a 15% payment; it would only receive the maximum (ceiling) payment of 10%.

Point-to-Point Measurement Methods

This describes the frequency and calculation of the index performance that will be used to influence your interest crediting value. The most common is the annual point-to-point, which means that the index value will be recorded on your annual anniversary date and then one year later it will be recorded again. The difference between the two recorded points will be the percent change used to calculate your interest payment.

The next most popular is the monthly point-to-point average. This means that the index will be measured each month and those twelve recorded values will be added up and divided by twelve. The resultant average is then used to calculate your interest payment for that period. There are many others, too many to describe in this book. Suffice it to say that you should seek professional assistance here.

Participation Rates

Participation rate is another way to limit the exposure

of the issuing insurance company. Participation rates define how much of your money is actually participating and gaining interest. For instance, a 50% participation rate implies that only 50% of your account balance amount is being used to calculate your interest payment. FIAs will often have no cap but only a 50% participation rate. Another way of looking at participation rates is that a 50% participation rate means you'll only get 1/2% of the positive interest amounts. That may be an easier way to remember how a participation rate can affect your gains.

That covers the basics, but as you work around FIAs, you will begin to see how the moving parts all align for a match to your type of investing style and income planning requirements. FIAs have gotten very creative lately with features such as multi-year point-to-point and a multi-year look back in which they look back two years and, if you deserve more interest for some reason, they give it to you. While it is safe to say that there are many FIA features and terms, we always say that the best FIA is one that has a floor above 0%, no cap or ceiling, and a 100% participation rate. Keep looking until you find it. If you have trouble locating one, we know of two.

Internal costs associated with an FIA are generally

accounted for internally within the insurance company. Caps and participation rate values instead of fees most commonly cover these, so the insurance company shares the risks with you. Another way that FIAs cover their costs is through the contract term. When you guarantee the insurance company that you will leave the money in place for a specified amount of time, it allows them to average their losses with the gains over time. Again, this is the insurance company taking on a portion of the risks with you.

But this also introduces the other downside of FIAs, and it is the same issue that all annuities have: the surrender charge. A surrender charge is a penalty charged by the issuing insurance company if you break the contract by withdrawing your money before the end of the contracted accumulation period. These periods can last anywhere from five to twelve years. As with CDs, the longer the term the greater the contracted rewards. Surrender charges are typically between 10% and 20% in the first year of a contract. Then they go down incrementally each year until they reach zero at or near the end of the term. If you had a ten-year annuity accumulation period and it started with a 20% surrender charge in year one, in year five you should expect the surrender charge to be about half of that (10%) or less, and decreasing even further every year thereafter. The surrender fees are always described in a chart, and this should be a minimum checkpoint for any FIA contract review.

Some opponents of annuities claim that any withdrawal triggers a surrender charge. This is typically not the case. Most annuities allow a 10% per year penalty-free withdrawal. This is especially convenient when you have your IRA or 401(k) in an FIA and you reach the age of seventy-and-a-half and are required to take the minimum annual withdrawals. These amounts are typically 7-8% and are easily withdrawn from your FIA without penalty.

While income from FIAs is not tax-free, if they are funded using non-IRS money (sometimes referred to as non-IRS qualified or non-qualified money), they can be tax-favored. This means that the withdrawals are treated like they are part principal (not taxed) and part interest (taxable). Thus, annuity payments can be taxed in smaller chunks, as they are withdrawn. The tax savings can be over 30% when compared to the typical IRA withdrawal. This can give you larger retirement income cash flow and minimize the effects of tax increases on your retirement income.

And what about FIAs and Future Proofing question number four—do they provide a wealth transfer when you pass away? Unlike the horror stories about annuities stealing the family inheritance, FIAs offer a myriad of life insurance riders to choose from. This next Future Proof comparison to stocks and bonds is a special feature that all FIAs should include. It goes by many names, but the usual name is a lifetime income rider or LIR. The LIR is an optional feature that can be added to all retirement-ready FIAs. The LIR creates a separate virtual account balance that grows each year by a fixed guaranteed percentage. Then at time of retirement you can choose either this value or your actual accumulated values, whichever is greater. And here is the best part: during retirement you will receive annual payments from that account for as long as you live—there is no way to outlive this money. And if you are married, you can choose a slightly reduced annual payment and have it last for as long as either of you are alive. This lifetime income rider can even be applied to your current IRA and 401(k) funds if you can roll them over soon enough. This is the epitome of Future Proofing against living too long and outliving your money!

And for all those Baby Boomers who want to retain full control during the pension payout phase, today's FIAs provide the option at any time during your retirement years to pull up stakes and withdraw all your remaining money in a lump sum if desired. The FIA contracts have addressed this need, and many have now included this as part of the contract terms to help us overcome the "annuity retirement puzzle" irony and enjoy a safer retirement with more options.

So how do FIAs stack up against typical "risk and reward" stock market vehicles? Below you will see a hypothetical example of two investors who started in 2000 with $100,000 each. Each investor wanted to retire in ten years (2009). The first investor chose an FIA with a 7% cap, a 100% participation rate, and a 0% floor (a subpar FIA by today's standards). The second investor chose an indexed mutual fund claiming that it would match the index (impossible in the real world, but we will give them the benefit of the doubt for this illustration). The index selected was the S&P 500, and below is the actual performance and account values that these hypothetical investors would have expected.

As you can see, the FIA owner starts his retirement in a much better position. But one could argue with our

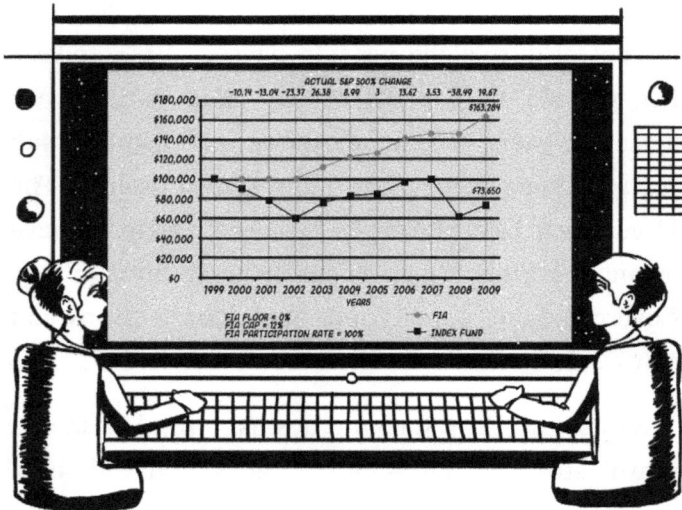

assessment and ask what would have happened in a real world example of a balanced stock portfolio versus an FIA portfolio over the last thirty years. This would be an enormous undertaking, and fortunately for us, Dr. Babbel of the Wharton School of Business has already done it. His research documents the difference between a balanced portfolio design and an FIA portfolio over the last thirty years. The result was that due to systematic risks and downside stock market losses that FIAs do not participate in, the FIA portfolio was the clear winner.[2] As

___

2   David F. Babbel, Jack Marrion, and Geoffrey VanderPal, "Real-World Index Annuity Returns," Wharton Financial Institutions Center (December 27, 2010).

Babel's research shows, FIAs beat a balanced portfolio hands-down as a vehicle for your retirement savings. Which one would you want to invest most heavily in?

CHAPTER 6

RISK, REWARD, AND RATIONING

On a barren, rocky planet like Mars, conserving resources is imperative. Even a self-sustaining colony must be attentive to its stockpiles of supplies in order to avoid running out of crucial components. The mission quartermasters spend hours in the colony's many warehouses, inventorying goods that were brought from Earth or sent from the lunar supply depot. To maintain a decent standard living for the colonists, the quartermasters must ensure adequate levels of water, clothing, hygiene products, and luxury goods.

In addition, the quartermasters must pay careful attention to the colony's renewable resources: goods manufactured on Mars and food grown in the farms,

THE MISSION QUARTERMASTERS CAREFULLY INVENTORY THE SUPPLIES THEY BROUGHT WITH THEM FROM EARTH.

orchards, and hydroponics laboratories. It's difficult to ship fresh food from the lunar base, so it's important to grow all fresh fruits, vegetables, and grains for a healthy diet on-site. They must guard against pests and plant diseases, as a single crop failure could prove disastrous to the food supply. And once the food has been harvested, they must ensure that it is stored properly to avoid spoilage and waste.

After gathering data on the state of all the colony's resources, the quartermasters will consult with chefs, nutritionists, and retailers to determine how much food, drink, clothing, luxury goods, and other supplies can be rationed to each colonist. Everyone will get the share they earn, but oversight is key if the settlement is to avert the crisis that would result from running out of essentials.

Just as a Mars colony is a lot like your retirement, managing food and supplies is analogous to managing your investments. Some assets, like bank accounts and CDs, are like supplies brought with you from Earth:

THEY MUST ALSO PAY CAREFUL ATTENTION TO THEIR RENEWABLE RESOURCES: THE CROPS GROWING IN THE COLONYS HYDROPONICS LAB.

THEY WILL USE THE DATA TO DETERMINE HOW MUCH FOOD THEY CAN RATION TO THE INHABITANTS OF THE COLONY WITHOUT RUNNING OUT OF SUPPLIES.

when they're gone, they're gone. Others are more like Martian-grown food or supplies sent from the moon: compound interest works its magic and continuously produces new funds. However, both types of assets must be carefully managed if you are to maintain your standard of living through retirement and leave something behind for your children. You have to know the best ways to use your life support assets if you're going to avoid running out of rations halfway through the journey.

If you ever get a chance to take a liberal arts college course titled "The Art of Negotiating," we strongly suggest it. Such a course had a profound effect on us. We expected guerrilla negotiation techniques, but instead it began with the premise that anything less than a win-win outcome was a failed negotiation. But the most memorable lesson was the hypothesis that before anyone makes a decision, the question is "routed" through the part of the brain located near the base of the neck. The instructor called this the "Old Brain." The Old Brain deals with instincts, and its main purpose is to make sure that whatever we do, we do not die from doing it. The Old Brain is what stops you from walking off cliffs or tells you to run from an angry bear. The Old Brain is stronger in some and weaker in others, but it is always there. If you expect anyone, even you, to make a decision, you must understand that it is always a life-or-death decision. As silly as that sounds, we have found it to be true every time we have tested it. In effect, while the frontal lobe can handle emotion or logic, the final decision must always pass the Old Brain's criteria: "Will I die?"

Why do we bring this up in a financial education book? Because we have found that the personal decision on how much liquidity someone needs is actually based within their Old Brain. It is not a logical decision. Over the years we have never met someone who could give us an exact answer on how much available cash or liquidity they need, but most can tell you how much they want. When pressed on "Why that amount?" the answers always gravitate around "I feel safe there" or "I don't know, I just do." I know that many have tried to come up with calculations like "X-months of income" and other formulas, but the truth is that there is no exact number that works for everyone. Everybody has a different need based on their Old Brain and its arbitrary safety levels.

This partially explains the street hermit who dies a millionaire. In his brain he always felt that he was going to die if he didn't have that money, yet he could never spend it while he lived seemingly penniless on the street. While this helps explain the condition, it also exhibits the main drawback. Money is supposed to be working for you 24/7/365. It should be constantly earning interest to offset inflation; otherwise you are always losing money to inflation and taxes, and that is not what the Old Brain wants. Somehow, today's financial gurus have convinced Americans that liquidity and growth are mutually exclusive. But the truth is that growing your wealth while your money is liquid and available is very possible. This is good for the Old Brain, but it sometimes takes a bit of work for the new brain to believe, not because it's rocket science, but because it challenges all that we were programmed to believe about how money works.

In our Future Proof investing courses, we teach our clients how to create retirement savings accounts that provide both liquidity and growth. We have named these accounts "Life Savings Accounts," or LSAs for short. An LSA is simply a retirement savings strategy that enables you to save your money with guaranteed and compounding interest rates with protection from losses and risks. LSA savings amounts can grow exponentially because of the compound interest, but it also offers liquidity and control to satisfy your Old Brain's available cash desires. The LSA strategy utilizes the very same financial principals that helped launch Disneyland, JC Penny, and McDonalds, just to name a few.

LSAs are quite simple in design, yet they provide benefits that are hard for most investors to wrap their brains around. Again, it's not because it's rocket science, but because it challenges all that we were programmed to believe about money. But trust us—this is how your banks and corporations handle their accounts. Money always works this way; they just hope that you won't figure it out and compete with them.

The first "True Money" concept that is hard to grasp is that LSAs continually grow through uninterrupted compounding. The word "uninterrupted" is the key. Unlike bank savings accounts or stock market accounts, LSAs are designed to never stop compounding interest, enabling your account balance to grow exponentially without losses from taxation or systematic market risks.

The second "True Money" concept is how LSAs provide accessibility to funds (liquidity) without interrupting the compound interest growth. We will explain this further, but in short, your LSA money is accessible and under your control through collateralization, not through withdrawals.

The third "True Money" concept is that an LSA can provide tax-free income during retirement. This is a byproduct of the liquidity feature above and will also be explained later in this chapter.

But before we dive too deep too soon, let's start at the beginning and work our way forward in our understanding of what a Life Savings Account is and what it can do for your retirement savings. To do this, lets go back to the Mars planning mission and use that to help us begin.

Imagine a spaceship full of colonists speeding toward Mars. Onboard is a storeroom where all the food that was brought from Earth is stockpiled. The interplanetary journey will take several years, so the quartermasters have to be careful to allocate the resources wisely. When they go to the storage room and remove food and deliver it to the colonists, this is like money coming into your hands from your monthly paycheck or income streams.

The first loss is due to food that spoils in storage—in your income example, this is perhaps taxes. You can put the remainder of what the quartermasters removed into a few different places, especially your two hydroponics labs on the ship. There, fruits and vegetables can be cultivated to produce more food, just like compound interest can create more money inside your LSA. These two labs represent the savings amounts designed to sustain your future lifestyle. Notice that it takes effort to plant and tend to these crops, just as it does to "plant" money and let it grow. This is not the natural flow of money for some, or for food on the ship; without careful planning, the colonists will simply eat all the food taken out of storage. Likewise, you have to expend energy and effort to save money—otherwise all of it will flow straight through to your current lifestyle.

But there's a difference between your two hydroponics labs. The first hydroponics lab represents the amount of your savings that you choose to expose to "risk and reward." The quartermasters suggested that you leave this lab unsecured and open. The option of someone eating or harvesting the produce from this lab is always there, but it also leaves the lab accessible to greater options and ideas through growth experiments, which could yield higher returns if successful. This lab represents the typical American's retirement savings that utilize stocks and bonds coupled with bank-based savings and liquidity. You can take money out of your savings anytime, and there are no guarantees or protections on your stocks and bonds portfolio. But the options of high yields, and/or considerable losses, are both available.

Conversely, you have decided not to harvest from your second hydroponics lab; instead, you replant the fruits and vegetables that it produces, which then exponentially grow more and more personal resources under your control. This lab is locked and protected from outsiders. This lab represents your Life Savings Account (LSA), where everything is safe, protected, and constantly growing with compound interest

The magic component of your LSA is compound interest, and the magic component of compound interest is time. More time to grow means more compounding, which means more wealth for you. So how often do you want to reset compounding? The answer is never. This illustrates why the other lab can never compound. "Risk and reward" gains and losses can never compound. Bank savings could possibly compound, but bank savings are taxed and withdrawn from, which resets the compound interest clock, and the vicious cycle continues.

In short, an LSA which is given the appropriate amount of time to grow will always outproduce a bank-based savings plan or a market-based investment plan. But the secret is to give it "time to grow."

While the possibility of exponential growth in our retirement savings accounts is something that many Americans dream about, it is just one of the three major advantages of an LSA. The other two unique features have to do with the liquidity and control that an LSA affords. But to help explain them for us, let's go back to

Chapter 6: Risk, Reward, and Rationing

our Mars planning mission again.

Imagine that while our spaceship is traveling towards Mars, you stumble across a secret. You discover that the quartermasters also have a protected, safe, and self-sufficient hydroponics lab just like yours, except it is much larger. Furthermore, all the food that they distribute to the travelers comes from this self-sustaining lab. While their lab is many times larger than yours, it works and grows the exact same way.

Life Savings Accounts share a similar secret. If you think about the concept of "money that makes more money," the banking institutions should come to mind first. Banks around the globe maximize the use of LSA-type accounts. In fact, American-regulated banks routinely maximize their use at up to 25% of their total balance sheet. Thus, 25% of the money they are loaning to you could be from their version of an LSA. Major corporations are also big users of these types of accounts. These corporate LSA accounts are how they fund the proverbial "golden parachutes" for their executives. Additionally, as stated earlier, the LSA strategy of funding was also the "seed money" used to launch Disneyland, JC Penny, and McDonalds, and that leads us to the second unique feature of your LSA:

liquidity, use, and control before retirement. That's right, before retirement! No waiting till 59 ½ (or later). LSAs are designed for liquidity, and that should make our Old Brains happy. But how LSAs provide liquidity is not something that your banker will teach you, so we will unveil the secret for you now.

Again, let's return to our Mars mission. Let's say the quartermasters notice that you have also created a protected and self-sustaining lab similar to theirs, and they notice it has experienced considerable growth already. They also realize that you are requiring less and less produce from them, and once you arrive at the Mars colony you may not need their produce anymore. They then confide in you that once they reach Mars they had planned on selling produce to the settlers from their self-sustaining lab. They therefore approach you with a proposal to combine your lab within theirs. In return, they will give you certain privileges and guarantees.

The "guarantee" is that your produce will grow within a guaranteed growth rate similar to a guaranteed minimum interest rate in a savings account. The "privilege" is that they will allow you to use your lab amount as collateral against future unplanned food needs. This means that unlike the other travelers, you can get extra food anytime you want just by asking. The only stipulation is that you can only take up to the amount you currently have in your lab. That way they could recoup the food amounts at any time if you do not pay it back for some reason.

If you are thinking this sounds like a pretty good deal, then you are going to love having an LSA. We already discussed exponential compound interest growth, and now you know that LSAs come with guaranteed minimum interest rates as well. But the truly interesting feature is the ability to get extra money any time you need it simply by using your LSA account balance as collateral.

This is immensely important because let's face it: the trials of life, such as college tuitions, weddings, and other planned and unplanned expenses, happen while we are saving for retirement. Paying for these events can force us to prematurely drain large portions of our savings or go deeper into debt. We know we need safety, guarantees, and growth, but we also need liquidity! How can we possibly get both? Liquidity through collaterization is what money-based professionals use, and it is the same thing that an LSA owner can use.

Liquidity through collateralization, or as we call it, the Wealth Creator Method, is a method unique to an LSA, and it helps you manage those "life happens" financial issues without draining your retirement savings or going deeper in debt. To properly the explain the Wealth Creator Method, we will introduce you to this financial truth: "You finance everything you buy. You either pay interest or you give up the ability to earn interest."

For example, let's assume that you need to make a purchase like a new car and you do not have enough money from monthly cash flow to make the purchase. You will need an infusion of money to make the purchase, and there are generally three methods to choose from.

First is the Debtor Method. A debtor who needs to buy a car will simply take out a loan to do so. In return the debtor pays compound interest to the bank. The Debtor Method is the one that all of the well-intentioned personal finance gurus warn you about. If the debtor needs money, they borrow money and work their way back to zero. Many people live a lifetime of frustration doing this over and over again. It's an inefficient purchasing strategy at best and a wealth stealing thief at worst.

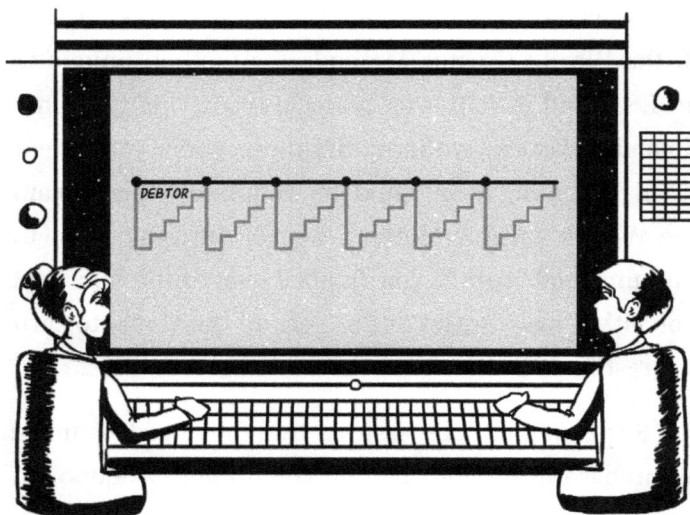

But how can we make purchases while avoiding debt? The number one answer is "pay cash," and this is what we call the Saver Method. But remember, we finance everything we buy; therefore, there are similar consequences when paying cash.

For example, let's assume that you had saved up the required amount of cash for the car and it is sitting in an account that is growing at a 3% or 4% compound interest rate. To buy the car, the saver withdraws all that money and gives it to the car dealer. At that point, the saver has forfeited all future annual compound interest gains on that money. The interest lost is called "opportunity

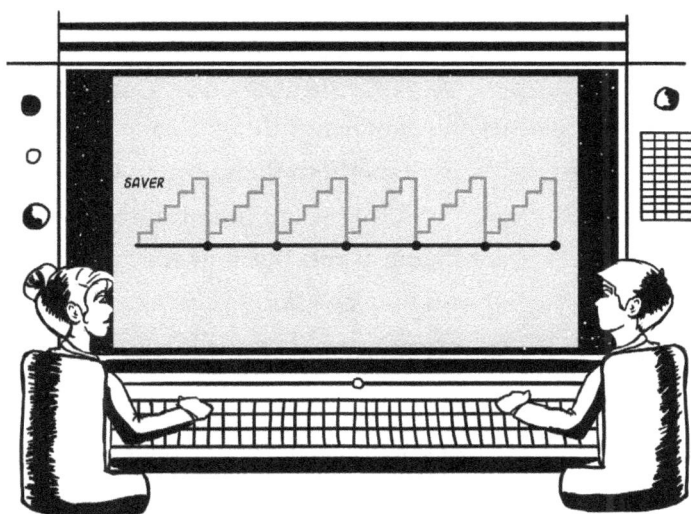

cost," and most get-out-of-debt gurus completely ignore it. We guess they hope you will too.

Now you see that we really do finance everything we buy. It is also interesting that mathematically, given equal interest rates, paying cash without ever repaying the amount back to the savings account will forfeit all future interest gains, and it will cost you the same amount as paying with a loan. If the saver does pay the amount back to themselves, the Saver Method can break even, but that does not create wealth—it just gets them back to square one. But let's admit it: paying cash carries less social stigmas while relieving the buyer from possible predatory payment plans and penalties, and that is a bonus over the Debtor Method.

Sadly, neither the debtor nor the saver method will ever create wealth. Both methods doom you to the same cycle over and over, and that is not financial freedom—it's just a different financial rut. But now that you have been enlightened, you may be asking yourself, "Is there a third way?" The answer is yes! It is the Wealth Creator method, the LSA.

The wealth creator uses a Life Savings Account to grow their money 24/7/365 through compound interest. They do this over a lifetime by never draining or withdrawing from the account. Instead, when they need to buy something, they go to the financial institution where their LSA is being held and request money for the purchase. Similar to the quartermaster's collateralization privilege, LSA owners accept the money, and an equal lien against their account balance with simple interest that is well below market rates, as well as unstructured payments. "Simple interest" means a once annual interest amount on the outstanding loan balance, and the interest rate is well below what others without collateral could demand. This is vastly different from the daily compounded interest charged to a debtor

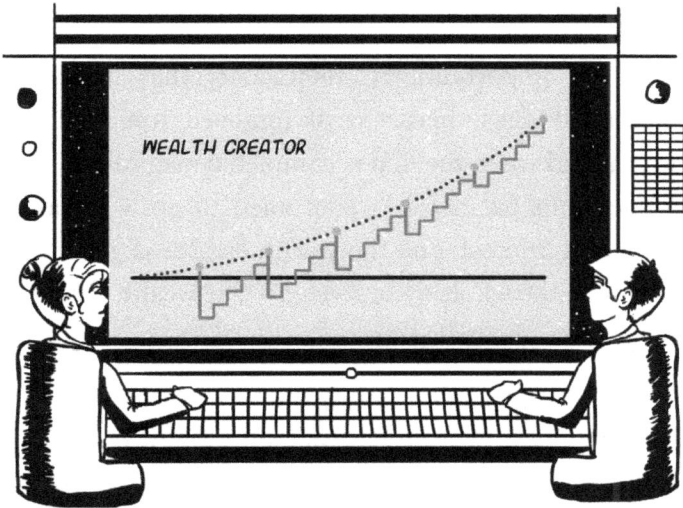

or the compounded opportunity cost to the saver. "Unstructured" means that since your account balance is being held as collateral, there are never any required payment schedules or penalties. This unstructured benefit is also enjoyed by the saver, but the debtor never enjoys this freedom.

Moreover, 100% of any repayments made will reduce the outstanding lien by that exact amount, reducing the annual simple interest that may be charged at year end. But most importantly, if the LSA is large enough and old enough, the compound interest growth within the Life Savings Account will dwarf the simple interest charges to the point where they are all but insignificant.

It is important to remember that properly maintained LSA funds are never removed from the LSA. Thus, if and when the lien is completely paid down, the LSA account balance has continued to grow through compound interest, and the wealth creator is wealthier than when the whole cycle started—true wealth creation and no more financial ruts.

Again, the magic component of the LSA and the Wealth Creator Method is compound interest, and the magic component of compound interest is time. More

The Debtor		The Saver			The Wealth Creator	
Bank loan with 6% interest, amortization over 5 years, balance owed amortization	6% interest cost	Pay with cash, 4% opportunity cost over 5 years, fund balance being "repaid"	4% opportunity cost on remainder not yet returned	4% gains on repaid funds	Liquidity through collateralization, 4% gains annually, account balance continues to grow	3% simple interest costs on remainder not yet returned
$10,000.00	$0.00	$0.00	$400.00	$0.00	$10,000.00	$300.00
$8,231.90	$551.90	$1,984.00	$319.84	$79.36	$10,400.00	$239.88
$6,354.89	$442.86	$3,988.00	$239.68	$159.52	$10,816.00	$179.76
$4,362.03	$327.08	$5,992.00	$159.52	$239.68	$11,248.64	$119.64
$2,246.27	$204.17	$7,996.00	$79.36	$319.84	$11,698.59	$59.52
$0.00	$73.67	$10,000.00	$0.00	$400.00	$12,166.53	$0.00
	$1,599.68			$1,198.40	$1,198.40	Gain: $2,166.53	$898.80
	Net: -$1,599.68				Net: $0.00		Net: $1,267.73
	Bad				Better		Best

The purchase price is $10,000. This scenario assumes a 6% debt interest, 4% interest gains, and a 3% simple interest lien rate. Both scenarios also assume a monthly "repayment" from current cash flow.

1. Debtor Mandatory Repayment = $193/month for 60 months
2. Saver Unstructured (Optional) Repayment = $167/month for 60 months
3. Wealth Creator Unstructured (Optional) Repayment = $167/month for 60 months

time means more compounding, which means more wealth for you. So how often do you want to reset compounding? The answer is never. So never directly take money out of your LSA—let it compound and simply use it as collateral to gain simple and advantaged terms.

Before we move on to our next concept, let's take a few moments and compare these three methods of buying, borrowing, and paying for major capital purchases.

How to Buy:

- Debtor: Works to spend, no savings, earns no interest, pays interest

- Saver: Saves to avoid paying interest, practices delayed gratification, earns interest on savings, pays cash and forfeits future interest and the power of compound interest by restarting the clock to zero

- Wealth Creator (LSA): Saves similar to the saver but uses other people's money to maximize efficiency, earns compound interest while collateralizing for purchases (leverages LSA retirement savings amounts as a security/collateral against purchase)

How to Borrow: (It will surprise some to know that all three borrow.)

- Debtor: Works to spend, borrows from lender at highest market rates using future earning potential as collateral

- Saver: Saves to avoid paying interest, borrows from self, thereby reducing current collateral position and resetting compounding (We've known a few people who pay cash and systematically put the money back using cash flow, but they never put back all the interest they lost while they had the money out of the account. But even if they did, those gains came from a reduced lifestyle, not compound interest gains, and that's a problem. Savers lose interest growth, and this is opportunity cost.)

- Wealth Creator (LSA): Saves and uses other people's money to maximize efficiency, borrows from lender at negotiated and low simple interest annual rates (not compounded daily rates like debtor) using own money only as collateral, so it continues to earn uninterrupted compounding growth (They can always look for the best deals/opportunities out there and get them before the saver or debtor because they always have access to funding.)

How to Pay:

- Debtor: Works to spend and makes payments to the lender at the highest market rates

- Saver: Saves to avoid paying interest, makes payments to self to get back to where they were before the purchase, giving up the interest their money would have earned (They may say they don't have payments, but to get back to where they were before, they're going to have to make payments, even if they're paid to themselves.)

- Wealth Creator (LSA): Saves and uses other people's money to maximize efficiency, makes unstructured payments to chosen lender, allowing their own money to earn uninterrupted compound interest growth, maximizing the growth of their retirement savings amounts while still satisfying life's liquidity needs

At this point, some readers may be experiencing disorientation because they just can't believe what they have just read. This is sometimes due to the marketing and "paid programming" by our bankers, "Financial

Bobble Heads," and "Wall Street Gurus." If this is you, we encourage you to re-read the preceding paragraphs with an open and inquisitive mindset. But always remember this: you must consider all the costs before any capital outlay, and that includes both interest and opportunity cost. It's not just what you pay for; it's also how you pay for it.

Almost universally, people who see this information for the first time struggle to accept that paying cash and taking out a loan is "exactly the same but completely different." They are both financial ruts and wealth stealers; they just start in a different direction. Meanwhile, an LSA strategy of leverage and collateral for preferred and simple terms with easy accessibility to funding is a far superior method that actually grows your wealth while you fund those "life happens" events. Yes, you can have liquidity and uninterrupted growth after all!

At our Future Proof courses, we teach our students and clients how to maximize and maintain their LSAs during their pre- and post-retirement years. Real estate investors leverage their LSA to obtain the funding for income properties and similar investments. Business owners free themselves from dictatorial bankers by using their LSAs as their line of credit funding. College-bound families use their LSA retirement funding to pay tuition costs without taking out predatory loans or strapping their kids with thirty years of payments. And one of the most common uses of the LSA's living liquidity benefits is the periodic purchase of automobiles. Imagine no more loan applications or bank inspectors, no more begging for a loan, no more credit card debt!

Students and clients in our Future Proof courses also learn how to employ an advanced banking industry concept called "the Velocity of Money" to grow wealth even faster. Velocity of Money is how banks use your single dollar in multiple loans to create multiple income streams. Inside your LSA, we teach you how to create your own personal velocity engine, but this is an advanced strategy, and we will not have the time or space to cover it adequately here.

The lifetime use of your LSA funds can provide true financial freedom, but as powerful as an LSA is before retirement, the LSA benefits during retirement are just as powerful, and that is our next topic.

Let's return to our Mars mission and the contract offered by the quartermasters. The quartermasters

Chapter 6: Risk, Reward, and Rationing

proposed a contract that offered access to additional food whenever needed using your reserves as collateral. They also guaranteed you a minimum growth rate. But you know that Mars is the real destination, and while you are there, you will need your food even more. You also know that food spoilage is on the rise, and just like taxes, spoilage is expected to be worse in the future. So, after reviewing your options, you counteroffer with a desire to obtain a guarantee on the amount of food you will receive once you land on Mars. Additionally, because spoilage can seriously erode how much of your food is actually useable, you ask for some protection against possible increases in spoilage.

Your quartermasters respond to your demands almost immediately, as if they have done this before. They reiterate the guaranteed growth rate they previously promised. Using that rate they can accurately project the minimum size of your food reserves upon arrival on the red planet. Then, using that same guaranteed growth rate, they calculate exactly how fast it will continue to grow after you arrive. This lump sum plus a guaranteed growth rate gives an accurate projection of how much food can be withdrawn for the thirty years or more that you are on Mars without running out of resources.

This intrigues you because in your other lab that has no protections and no guaranteed growth rate, the idea of accurately projecting what your reserves will be at any given time is impossible.

As for the risk of spoilage increases, the quartermasters offer a contract clause that guarantees your food will be spoilage free as long as you continue to use the collateralization method from the original contract terms. In other words, as long as you have collateral in your lab, they will give you food that is spoilage free.

A good contract just got better! First, the guaranteed minimum interest rate allows the LSA owner to easily predict how much money will be in the account at almost any given time, especially at time of retirement. Try doing that with a balanced portfolio of stocks and bonds. You might be able to try this with bank CDs, but LSA interest rates are currently 300-400% greater than CD's, and unlike a CD, an LSA grows tax-deferred. Secondly, probably the most interesting feature of your LSA is that during retirement you can get your retirement funding amounts tax-free.

This is very important because in the same way that

spoilage can reduce the amount of your useable food amounts, taxation can reduce the amount of useable retirement income. In previous chapters we discussed the risk that IRS and state income tax rates might grow progressively worse. Entitlement programs, bailouts, and a skyrocketing national debt almost guarantee that taxation will increase in our future. And unfortunately, it will most likely increase dramatically. If and when this happens, your retirement could be delayed, devastated, or both.

Let's take a moment and calculate how much "spoilage" or taxation could affect your retirement. Let's use a thirty-year retirement for this example. Using a calculator, enter the annual income that you enjoy right now and multiply by thirty. Based on inflation, this will be pretty close to the total amount of pre-tax money you will need during retirement. Now let's assume a 25% tax rate during retirement. Using the calculator again, subtract 25%. That was a pretty big reduction, wasn't it? Furthermore, we believe tax rates are going to increase to near record levels by the time we retire, so we would subtract 35% or more as our predicted tax rate during retirement. But whatever percentage you may choose to subtract for taxes, divide that result by thirty, and this will display your annual after taxes useable income during retirement. Which number would you rather have during retirement, the before taxes amount or the after taxes amount?

If you chose the before taxes amount, you should include an LSA as part of your retirement savings strategy. The LSA Wealth Creator Method enables retirees to leverage funding against their compound interest bearing and exponentially growing LSA balances. Since the terms of the funding are always unstructured, the funding amounts received do not mandate repayment schedules or penalties. Couple this with the fact that your LSA account balance is now growing exponentially, the annual one-time simple interest on the lien becomes insignificant in comparison to the annual compound interest growth. Thus, you are able to live off the funding amounts for the rest of your life without ever actually withdrawing money from your LSA and resetting the compound interest growth.

Notice that since you have not made any withdrawals, the retirement funding from your LSA liens is not taxable because it is not income. But the money you receive can be used for whatever you want to spend it on. Paycheck or "play-check," it's your choice, and they are not subject to ordinary income tax or capital gains tax, whatever those rates may be during your retirement. This is how LSA owners enjoy tax-free retirement funding.

Tax-free income during retirement can be calculated and predicted for any LSA owner. It is also one of the areas that we help our students and clients to mathematically project at our Future Proof courses.

While LSAs can be your best retirement savings and retirement funding option, the last LSA concept we are going to cover might be the most powerful of all. To explain, let's return to our Mars mission one final time.

The latest offer from the quartermasters gave you protection from future spoilage increases with predictable reserve balances during and before arrival. And while this is extremely impressive, the ease that your quartermasters have responded to your demands makes you wonder if your quartermasters haven't done this all before. Nonetheless, you decide to ask for one more item.

You've calculated that the guaranteed growth rate they offered you is the same growth rate that you achieved in your little lab. With all the resources that the quartermasters have at their disposal, they should at least double or triple what you achieved. This means that even though you will profit well from the agreement, they too will profit, but five or ten times more. So you make your final request. On top of all the other terms offered, you ask that if you pass away for any reason, the quartermaster must pay your heirs five times what your food reserves are at that time.

Once again, the quartermasters seem unruffled and respond immediately, as if they have done all this before. They agree to your request of fivefold payment, but minus any unpaid food advances. They also prescribe that if you pass away before a predetermined accumulation time period, they will reduce the amount paid proportionately.

However, they have essentially agreed to all your terms, and a good contract just got great! If anything happens to you, your heirs will receive up to five times your reserves. While on Mars, you are protected from spoilage losses and are guaranteed a predictable flow of food. And best of all, before you get to Mars you get a guaranteed growth rate and can request extra food anytime you need it. This is better than you ever thought possible, and there is just one thing left to do: sign the contract! That night, when you check into your sleeping pod, you sleep soundly and deeply. You feel content knowing that all your planning and hard work will provide a better life for you and your family—just like the owner of a properly established and maintained LSA.

Exactly like the quartermasters who seem to have done this all before, the LSA concepts and strategies are not new. They have been in use by the fortunate few for well over a hundred years. LSAs have shown themselves under many different names, but they always work in basically the same manner: liquidity through collateralization, uninterrupted compound interest, and a leveraged inheritance for your heirs. You sleep well and your Old Brain feels good again!

Now let's talk about our available options for storing and maintaining our Life Savings Account. This used to be a lengthy process until we began using the Future Proof Scorecard system. By simply answering yes or no to the required features, you can quickly and easily narrow down your best choice. The top row lists all the usual choices and the left-hand column lists the minimum requirements needed to establish and maintain an effective LSA account. As you can quickly see, one column seems to have the most positives.

Not surprising, for over a hundred years now, permanent life insurance has over and over again proven itself to be the best carrier for Life Savings Accounts. But not just any permanent life insurance policy—it must be a specific type. A proper LSA policy must be one that is over-funded, designed for collateral use, and preferably dividend paying or equivalent. Coincidentally, this policy type can be seen on almost every corporate bank financial statement. It will be listed as BOLI, which stands for bank-owned life insurance. As mentioned before, if you think about the idea of "money that generates more money," the banks should come to mind first, and they maximize their BOLI use at up to 25% of their total balance sheet. Not to be outdone, major corporations

Future Proof Scorecard

	Permanent Life Insurance	IRA/401(k)	Roth IRA	Home/Real Estate	Savings/CDs	Stocks/Bonds/Mutual Funds	Fixed Annuities
Protected Capital (no losses)	Yes	No	No	No	Yes	No	Yes
Liquidity and Control	Yes	Possible with Loan or Surrender	Possible with Loan or Surrender	Possible with Home Equity Loan	Yes	Yes	Yes, with Possible Penalties
Exposure to Risks and Unpredictable Losses	No	Yes	Yes	Yes	No	Yes	No
Tax-Deferred Gains	Yes	Yes	Yes	Yes	No	Yes	Yes
Tax-Free Distribution	Yes	No	Yes	IRS Limits	No	No	No
Contribution Limits	No	Yes	Yes	No	FDIC Limits	No	No
Compound Interest Growth	Yes	No	No	No	Yes	No	Yes
Excessive Fees	No	Sometimes	Sometimes	No	Sometimes	Sometimes	Sometimes
Tax-Free Transfer to Heirs	Yes	No	No	IRS Limits	No	No	Possible

are also big users of these types of accounts. These amounts are listed on corporate balance sheets a COLI, which stands for corporate-owned life insurance. COLI is how they fund the proverbial "golden parachutes" for their executives, as well as funding options for their line of credit needs.

But beware: these LSA-enabled policies do not just exist; they must be designed. A qualified and trained professional must individually design each policy for each case. Unfortunately, thanks to the booming 80s and 90s stock market, the art of policy design was discarded and replaced by the stock market mantra of "buy term

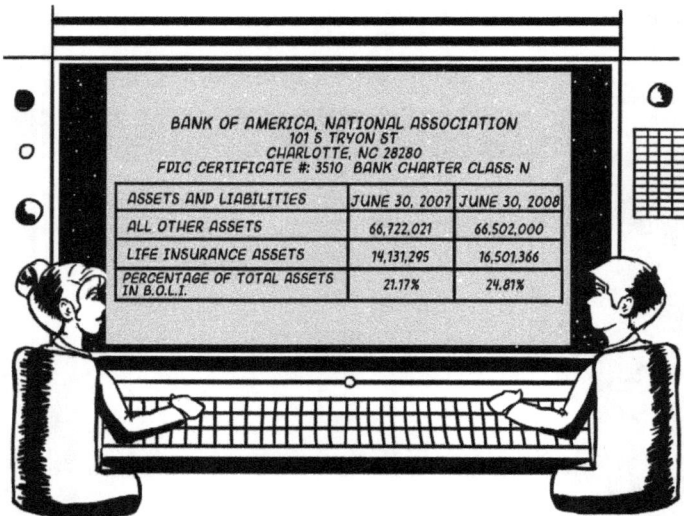

ASSETS AND LIABILITIES	JUNE 30, 2007	JUNE 30, 2008
ALL OTHER ASSETS	66,722,021	66,502,000
LIFE INSURANCE ASSETS	14,131,295	16,501,366
PERCENTAGE OF TOTAL ASSETS IN B.O.L.I.	21.17%	24.81%

BANK OF AMERICA, NATIONAL ASSOCIATION
101 S TRYON ST
CHARLOTTE, NC 28280
FDIC CERTIFICATE #: 3510 BANK CHARTER CLASS: N

and invest the rest." This strategy and mantra began in the early 80s as a ploy to minimize the client's insurance spending and therefore maximize the amounts that can be funneled into stocks and bonds.

On the surface you would think that insurance companies would resist this mantra, but the opposite is true. This is because over 95% of all term policies expire before paying out a death benefit. For the insurance companies it is a constant flow of money coming in and virtually no money going back out. That's like printing money; unfortunately, it is our money they are taking. So it's not surprising that during this time period, life insurance salesman were all being trained (and paid additional incentives) to sell these minimum-funded life insurance policies that expire after a predetermined term—hence the name "term policy."

This mantra also became a favorite of insurance salesmen because the insurance companies began paying additional incentives to sell these types of policies, and everyone knows that "compensation dictates behavior." To make matters worse, the typical insurance salesman is almost trained to design poorly performing permanent life insurance policies when asked about them, because this makes their term policies look more attractive. These

Chapter 6: Risk, Reward, and Rationing

Trojan Horse policy designs tout only the death benefit and never grow wealth like an LSA is designed to do. In some ways we can agree with the "Financial Bobble Heads," when they rant and rave that life insurance can be a terrible investment. As the saying goes, "Figures never lie—but liars can figure."

Today, less than 5% of all licensed insurance representatives know what an LSA is, let alone how to design one. When you combine this with the paid programming by Wall Street and the IRS over the last twenty years, you begin to realize why so many financial gurus and talking heads are oblivious to the Wealth Creator Method and how properly designed, permanent life insurance policies are the perfect carrier for your Life Savings Accounts. Meanwhile, our banks and major corporations maximize their use and the rich get richer.

Again, the LSA concept and strategy is not new. We wish we could claim that we invented this new wealth creation and perpetuation strategy, but that would be a lie. In fact, if you have ever heard the term "trust fund baby," then you probably already know of the benefits of this strategy—you just did not know how it worked.

A trust fund is usually established through

specifically designed and overfunded permanent life insurance policies when the child is still an infant. The trust fund policies grow compounded and exponentially for the next eighteen to twenty years. Then, when the child comes of age, they are taught how to leverage the account, use it only as collateral for funding, and never drain it. Proper management of this funding enables them to continue to grow wealth and never run out of money their whole life. Next, the trust fund children are taught that when they pass away, the money is transferred to their heirs as a death benefit. The new amounts are usually transferred tax-free, fivefold larger, and available to perpetuate the whole cycle for the next generation.

And the next time you are walking through a zoo or museum and you see a plaque that reads something like "Donated by the Jones Family Foundation," the chances are very high that the donation was made from an LSA policy type called a Charitable Family Foundation Trust. These trusts are formed as non-profit trusts that the heirs can live off of, tax-free, as long as they make periodic charitable contributions.

But again, creating and maintaining an LSA-suitable permanent life insurance policy like this is not as simple as opening a bank account or buying a term life insurance policy. Trust fund families routinely employ highly paid money managers and wealth advisors to do this for them. You too should seek the assistance of a qualified and specially trained professional to help you and your family. Once established, your financial future will get infinitely brighter.

In our Future Proof classes and courses we explain in detail how insurance policies operate and all the levers and knobs to use when creating and maintaining them as your LSA carrier. But we wanted to touch on the major points for our readers who may not have attended one of our classes yet.

The way that permanent life insurance works as an LSA carrier starts with something called "cash value." When you put money in your policy, the insurance company calls that a premium payment. All premiums that "overfund" the policy are stored in a savings account-type holder called "cash value." Initially, you probably won't have access to 100% of all the resources. You will probably have access to somewhere around 80%-90%, depending on the company and the product design. The main reason they hold a reserve is to create a shield for the death benefit, to make sure that everything you want to happen can happen. No other product listed on our Future Proof Scorecard offers the death benefit for your heirs or charities. You have to live long enough to put money away, but in the event of an early death, the life insurance death proceeds automatically take care of your family or charity. What a great position! It makes the Old Brain feel all warm and fuzzy inside.

But it's not just the death benefit we're looking at; we want growth and access to capital. For growth, the insurance policy is a contract between yourself and the insurance carrier. In that contract will be the minimum interest guarantees that you can expect. Typically these are from 3-5%, depending on the carrier and the policy design. Additional growth is realized in the non-guaranteed form of dividend payments into your cash value account. The annual growth from dividends is historically one to three percentage points of your annual cash value amounts. However, dividends are always based on the annual performance of the insurance carrier, so they are not guaranteed. Thus, a properly structured LSA can expect to gain 3-5% annual interest plus 1-3% dividend each year, compounded, and never exposed to systematic risks. The additional feature is that cash value growth is tax-deferred, so the compounding happens without the annual drag of taxes like CDs and bank accounts suffer from.

But we also need liquidity through collateralization, so let's look at how an LSA-enabled life insurance policy would work for us on that all-important point. Let's assume you have money in your cash value balance and you need to buy a car. You can contact the insurance company any time you want to request the funds needed and enable a lien against your collateral capacity (cash value amount - reserve amount - outstanding lien amounts = current collateral capacity). However, you are the owner of the cash value, which can be used as collateral anywhere, so you want to make sure that you're shopping for the best deal. It may not always be the insurance carrier, but most times it does end up that way because you receive the insurance company protections and unstructured repayments. But again, you want to remember that you own the collateral and you are the one who is in control.

Assuming we choose the insurance company for the funds needed, you request the funds and accept a policy lien against your cash value. In effect, you will borrow from the insurance company. They will in turn look in your account and see if you have enough collateral capacity available. If the answer is yes, then they will supply you with the requested funds and strike an equal lien against your collateral position.

From then on, you can decide to make non-structured payments, meaning you pick the amount and time of repayment. No penalties, no late fees, no credit collection departments.—just full financial control. You can repeat the cycle over and over again, as often as you want. And remember, you never stop gaining interest on your cash value amounts. You achieve uninterrupted compounding with full liquidity and control. Who told us this was impossible?

In our Future Proof courses, our clients and students also learn what you can do with the extra cash flow you now have, if and when the lien is re-paid and removed. We recommend that you further over-fund your life insurance contract to the next highest level. When you're full, look for another life insurance contract where you can over-fund another policy and multiply the whole process for greater wealth and financial freedom.

Last, but definitely not least, imagine for a minute what your Future Proof retirement funding inside of a permanent life insurance policy has inherently created. When properly designed and maintained, your beneficiaries will receive a tax-free death benefit that is many times larger than all that you have saved. And since the IRS requires the death benefit to be a prescribed level above your cash value amounts in order to remain tax-free, your heirs can always count on a guaranteed, leveraged inheritance if anything were to happen to you.

With an LSA providing liquidity and growth, predictable and tax-free retirement funding, and the world's best vehicle to provide your heirs or charities with a leveraged inheritance, there is just one more thing to do: ask yourself why you don't have one already!

CHAPTER 7

THE NEXT GENERATION

In truth, the careful planning of the settlement was never for the benefit of the Mars colonists alone. Mission control had a much longer vision of the future in mind. Once the colony became self-sustaining, it could begin to grow. Other domes were established on the surface of the red planet, and they all worked together toward the common goal of Martian prosperity. Before the original colonists died off, they could rest assured of leaving behind thriving communities. The future of humanity on Mars was now secure.

But that wasn't all. With prosperity came new technologies and population growth. The colonists' children built on their parents ideas and invented faster

Chapter 7: The Next Generation

THE SUCCESS OF THE MARS COLONY ALLOWED THE COLONISTS' CHILDREN TO EXPLORE AND COLONIZE THE REST OF THE SOLAR SYSTEM AND BEYOND.

methods of space travel. Thanks to their forebears, they had the resources and knowhow to expand toward the next frontier: other planets. Taking with them supplies grown and manufactured on Mars, the next generation blasted off for the rest of the solar system—and beyond.

In the depths of space, they encountered challenges their parents never could have dreamed of. They landed on planets that were friendly to human habitation and inhospitable rocks devoid of water and air. They encountered new dangers and new forms of life that stretched their capacity to survive and thrive.

But wherever they went in this galaxy or others, they always managed to settle and build new colonies.

Within a few generations, a vast network of self-sufficient human colonies stretched from Venus to the Alpha Centauri galaxy 4.37 light years away. And these brave explorers owed their success to the foresight and planning of their pioneer parents and their groundbreaking colony on the red planet.

Your investments aren't only for you and your retirement. At their best, they're also for the benefit of your children and grandchildren. Aspire to something greater. Build a Life Savings Account you can hand off to your children, and that they can maintain to hand off to their children. Start the legacy of intergenerational wealth in your family. Your descendants will thank you for the opportunities you create for them.

Chapter 7: The Next Generation

"A good man leaves an inheritance to his children's children, but the sinner's wealth is laid up for the righteous." —Proverbs 13:22

What would you call a neighbor of yours who snuck off in the middle of the night, leaving their kids, spouse, and a baby granddaughter forever with no visible means of support and a pile of debt? What adjectives would you use to describe this person?

Now, what would you call a neighbor of yours who died in the middle of the night, leaving their kids, spouse, and a baby granddaughter forever with no visible means of support and a pile of debt? What adjectives would you use for them? The adjectives and emotions would be a little different, but the end results would be exactly the same.

Now, what if we took that second scenario but this person left their family a large life insurance policy death benefit that paid off all debts and created enough money for a comfortable lifestyle for the rest of their lives? What would you call the person this time? We would most likely use phrases such as "thoughtful spouse," "wise parent," or "loving grandparent." That gift of love to their family, and maybe even to their favorite charity, expresses that their commitment to family and charity did not end with their last breath.

We know this discussion is sensitive, but it is not meant to be about death as much as it is about wisdom. Wisdom is not knowledge. There are many intelligent people out there who are not very wise. Wisdom is the combination of knowledge and experience. Knowledge that is not tested against time can be foolish. Knowledge that passes the tests of time becomes wisdom.

The questions above are an attempt to impart a bit of wisdom to a Boomer generation that has historically ignored their own mortality. We Boomers will begin facing our mortality much later than our parents and grandparents had to. At age sixty-five we may still be looking at another twenty to thirty years of living. But as sure as the fact that one day we took our first breath, we will someday take our last. And after your last breath, will you be called a "thoughtful spouse," "wise parent," "loving grandparent," or even "generous benefactor"? If you are a Future Proof investor, then you have built a wise foundation for intergenerational wealth for your heirs and charities.

Future Proof planning enables you to create this

kind of legacy without spending any more than you would have using IRAs, 401(k)s, stocks, bonds, or CDs for your retirement plan. Your Future Proof retirement plan leverages the inherent features of life insurance vehicles for your Future Proof planning. And the most powerful feature might just be the concluding payout of the death benefit to your heirs upon your passing. This death benefit can even be structured to be exempt from IRS taxation, creating a tax-free wealth transfer to your heirs and/or favorite charities. But even if the taxman does get at your death benefits, Future Proof planning is still a magnitude better for you and your heirs.

Why is that? First you must understand what a death tax is and does. Let's take a moment and think about who will be the first person to enter the scene after your last breath is taken and your wealth is being distributed to your heirs and your chosen charities: the taxman. That's right—the IRS estate taxes must be paid first. The estate tax is the portion of your belongings that the IRS now considers to be theirs due solely to the fact that you passed on. This portion, which we refer to as the IRS death tax, must be paid first, before your heirs or your charities can ever receive theirs. Currently the estate tax exemption threshold is fluctuating between one and

FAMOUS ESTATES

	GROSS ESTATE	SETTLEMENT COST	NET ESTATE	PERCENT SHRINKAGE
ELVIS PRESLEY	$10,165,434	$7,374,635	$2,790,799	73%
WILLIAM BOEING	$22,386,158	$10,589,748	$11,796,410	47%
ALWIN ERNST,CPA	$12,642,431	$7,124,112	$5,518,319	56%
MARILYN MONROE	$819,716	$448,750	$370,426	55%
NELSON EDDY	$472,715	$109,990	$362,725	23%
'GABBY' HAYES	$111,327	$21,963	$89,364	20%

SOURCE:BASED ON PUBLIC PROBATE RECORDS.

five million dollars, and the tax rate is 50%. During the Carter presidency the exemption threshold hovered near $360,000 dollars, and the death tax rate was also 50%. If you passed away during that time, approximately 50% of all your wealth above $360,000 was owed to the IRS before your heirs or charities could even begin to receive their portion. The threshold and rate levels change with each administration, but wealthy families still use the same Future Proof vehicles to mitigate these death taxes, even during a Carter year or the administrations of any impersonators who may come along in the future.

The next entity that will try to enter the scene will

be the probate court. Probate courts are the hands and feet of the IRS at the local level. Once you pass away, all assets become the property of the probate court unless you have a surviving spouse or trust. This can be very problematic for the heirs after the second spouse passes. In this case, the only way for your kids or charities to receive your gift to them is by petitioning the probates to execute the wishes from your will. This process takes weeks or months to complete, as the probate court makes sure that the IRS death taxes are paid first, followed by their deductions for the probate court costs. Then, and only then, will they discuss your wishes for the remainder with your heirs.

Contrast this probate process with a Future Proof financial plan, which seamlessly distributes your death benefit payouts to your heirs. Life insurance death benefits are automatically distributed per your beneficiary designations without ever going through probate. Your final wishes are contractually executed with no probate fees or probate interpretation hassles.

Now let's forget Future Proof planning for a minute and examine the common man's practice of using IRAs, stocks, and CDs for retirement planning, analyzing how it all gets distributed after your demise. First, let's examine the IRS favorite, the IRA. All funds in an IRA are passed on to your beneficiaries, but the proceeds are taxed at the ordinary income tax rate of your heirs. Unfortunately for them, they are probably in the highest tax bracket they have ever been in, since it usually occurs when they are at the peak of their earning years. It gets worse if your estate value exceeds the current death tax threshold. In that case, before your heirs get anything, the death tax of 50% would be extracted.

Let's do a simple example. Say your home is worth $360,000 and you have $100,000 in an IRA. And just your luck, you die during the Carter era or some other administration in the future that duplicates those death tax exemption levels and rates. The home value puts you over the threshold, so all the rest of your assets are subject to the 50% death tax. Your heirs would then be eligible for only $50,000 of your $100,000 IRA. Next, assume your heir is paying a 30% nominal income tax rate. This means that Uncle Sam would assess a $15,000 tax bill on their $50,000 inheritance. Thus, for every $100,000 in an IRA, your heirs would only receive $35,000. The other $65,000 is taken by the taxman.

God forbid that your $100,000 is still in a 401(k) when you die. This can be even worse, as 401(k) money is first subject to the plan rules for early withdrawal, and then the remainder is subjected to the same fate as the IRA. Having intergenerational money in a 401(k) is even more problematic.

But what if you held it all in mutual funds or stocks and bonds? This changes the tax rate from the ordinary income tax rate (usually the highest) to the capital gains tax rate (usually lower). But the initial death tax loss of 50% is still there, and if the capital gains tax is only 15%, then your heirs will receive $42,500 in inheritance for every $100,000 left in the market. This is definitely better than an IRA, but it's not a desirable outcome, either.

Finally, let's imagine that same $100,000 in our bank in CDs and savings accounts. Hello probate court, and yes, the same 50% death tax. The complications increase, and the taxation is virtually the same as with the mutual funds above.

Now let's look at Future Proof planning using the same assumptions. Life insurance death benefits will most likely be taxed at the same death tax rate, but they avoid the income and/or capital gains tax. This leaves your Future Proof investing 15-30% better off, assuming that the $100,000 was all they received from the policy. But it isn't—we're getting to that.

Let's not forget the strategic planning that Future Proofing provides. Strategically, wealthy families think differently about money than the common man does. Wealthy families are always looking for ways to leverage their money, and one of the most widely used forms of leverage is the life insurance death benefit. For example, $100,000 in cash value can create two to five million dollars in death benefit for your heirs. This multiplication erases any parity assumed with stocks, banks, or IRAs.

Let's examine why. We will use that same $100,000, but this time it is cash value within an LSA. Assume the LSA provides a death benefit of just one million. Upon death, the IRS takes out the 50% death tax, and the remaining $500,000 is distributed to your heirs without income or capital gains tax. Compare this $500,000 inheritance to the banking and Wall Street-approved alternatives of $35,000 or $42,500 inheritance. This is an excellent example of why the rich get richer while the uninformed and misinformed do not.

While looking at the example above, you may think that the IRS would be very excited to have every

Chapter 7: The Next Generation

American practice Future Proof investing, since they received $500,000 in tax revenue instead of $65,000 on the same $100,000 asset. But the truth is that if the surviving spouse or heirs owned the policy instead of the deceased, there would be no estate tax due. This policy ownership planning can be used many different ways, which creates a love-hate relationship between the IRS and Future Proof investing strategies.

So why is it that many so-called financial planners spend so much time trying to reduce the $65,000 losses in what they call estate planning? Instead, they should plan how to pay $500,000 in taxes because the heirs receive $500,000 in inheritance! We would think that is proper estate planning, not trying to minimize how much of your $100,000 your heirs and charities will lose. You might ask why most financial planners are not Future Proof investing advisors. Again, follow the money. Every stockbroker works for a brokerage firm, and their job is to sell stocks and bonds first and foremost. While they are licensed and regulated, they are paid on commissions and fees. This is why they limit themselves to selling stocks and bonds for your estate planning.

A case in point was that recently a son and his

mother came to us because the mother was in her eighties and very financially troubled. When we looked at their documents we noticed that she had all her assets at one large and well-known bank. Furthermore, the family was very upset about the fact that the bulk of the money was in an annuity and the bank was telling them that they could not make changes to the annuity, and that they could suffer large penalties if they were to surrender the policy.

Knowing what we know, it was curious to us that the family was angry at the annuity but not the bank or their financial planner. Our office asked to step in because we saw some irregularities in the documentation, and when we called the bank to inquire about them we were told that they could not talk to us because all the assets were still in the name of the husband, and he was not present with us at that time. When we informed the bank's financial planner that the husband had passed away five years prior, he stumbled a bit before finally requesting a death certificate to prove it.

Once that issue was straightened out, we were able to uncover for the family that it wasn't just an annuity—it was the evil twin, a variable annuity. All this time, his mother's money was being exposed to stock market risks and was suffering numerous losses, yet here she was in financial trouble and desperately in need of those funds. Furthermore, the surrender charges on the variable annuity had nearly expired by that time, so there were negligible charges to liquidate the annuity and fix the problem. We were able to transfer her funds out of that bank, and we assure you that the family anger was no longer at an annuity.

If we had been able to correct this years earlier, the family may have had many more financial options, and the son could have expected a much larger inheritance while his mother enjoyed a much easier financial life. But at least the family is now a Future Proof investing family with a much brighter financial future

This example shows how typical financial advisors rarely inform their clients how life insurance can easily enable generations of wealth. We also fear that until the writing of this book, many people did not really understand the simplicity with which it can be done. Think back to the wealthy patriarch who creates a million dollar cash value life insurance policy on every newborn family member. The million dollars grows compounded every year for eighteen to twenty years, and when the children come of age, the policies are leveraged during their entire lifetimes for tax-free income using the LSA lien and collateralization concepts. This describes a typical "trust fund baby" scenario.

But it does not stop there. Wise families instill in their children the discipline to maintain the policy all their life so that upon their death, the policy pays another five times multiplication into the family wealth fund to fund new policies. There are literally thousands of real life families practicing this intergenerational wealth strategy every year. In fact, the next time you walk through a museum or a zoo and you see a plaque saying something like "Donated by the Smith Family Foundation," you can be fairly certain of the underlying wealth engine that they employed to enable this donation.

Meanwhile, the familiar tools of the common man—IRAs, 401(k)s, stocks, bonds, mutual funds, CDs, and savings accounts—do not provide leverage or multiplication. They are subject to more IRS taxes and create less wealth when you pass. This may be good enough for your annoying neighbor down the street, but ask yourself, "Is that what I want for my legacy?"

A properly established Future Proof retirement savings plan naturally includes an inheritance to your

Chapter 7: The Next Generation

heirs and charities that is many times larger than that which you were able to save during your lifetime. This will provide many benefits to those whom you love and those who love you. Not only does it mitigate tax issues and multiply wealth for your children and your children's children, it more importantly reduces complexity for them during a time of grieving. Become a Future Proof investor and begin anew to train your children well, and your legacy will be remembered forever!

CHAPTER 8

MISSION PLANNING

Mission control had debated for months. Every expert in every field had been consulted, and they were confident that they had the best information available to them. But examining information was one thing, and actually sitting down and making a plan was another thing entirely. Before they were willing to risk the lives and livelihoods of an entire crew of colonists, mission control wanted to be absolutely sure they had interpreted the data correctly and charted the best possible course for the mission. The future of humanity on Mars depended on the decisions they made. So they all took deep breaths, got out pencil and paper, and got to work making a plan.

Chapter 8: Mission Planning

Now you have learned how an LSA will provide you with liquidity and consistent growth, while an FIA can provide market-type growth without the risks usually associated with stock and bonds. We also discovered that during retirement, FIAs and LSAs provide predictable and consistent sources of tax-free and tax-favored income. These gains and income can keep up with inflation, all without the usual stock market losses that have hampered so many retirees in these volatile times. But best of all, you can have those income streams last for the rest of your life, just like the pensions of old—while maintaining complete control of your money.

Future Proofed investing can be the best financial strategy for millions of Americans, and possibly you as well. But the first question everyone has is, "How do I get started?" That is what we will cover in this chapter.

It is worth stating that the following steps are just the beginning. To really implement a proper future proof financial plan, you need the assistance of a qualified financial advisor, one who is licensed and trained in the insurance industry and specifically trained in FIAs and Life Savings Account structures and handling. Many of our clients also take our classes at local colleges and adult education centers. This grants them additional access to our qualified instructors, who help them get educated and begin implementing their Future Proof financial plan.

The first step in creating a Future Proof retirement plan is to decide from a very high level what portion of your retirement funds you wish to put into your future proof accounts. At this step it's not important to decide how much to keep liquid versus how much to put in growth; simply decide on the percentage of your total assets that you feel should be Future Proofed.

To do this, draw three "tanks" or columns on a piece of paper. At the top of the left-hand column/tank write "Safe and Liquid Fuels" or SL. This will represent the portion of your retirement savings that you would like to be stored in bank deposits and CDs. At the top of the right-hand column/tank write "Risky and Volatile Fuels" or RV. This will represent the portion of your retirement savings that you would like to remain exposed to systematic risks such as the stock and bond markets and other risk-and-reward based investments. At the top of the center column/tank write "Future Proof Fuels" or FP. This represents the portion you would like to be in Future Proof investments, an LSA and FIA combination tank.

Now, in each column/tank enter a percentage that represents the mix ratios that you feel comfortable with. The only requirement is that the sum of all three percentages equal 100%, representing your total financial picture.

There are several considerations for this step. To begin with, in the banking tank, remember that even though LSAs provide excellent liquidity, they are not designed for daily expenses. LSAs are designed for larger purchases and expenditures. Therefore, leaving a percentage in an ultra-liquid savings/checking account is generally a prudent choice. That being said, if you still desire to leave some of your assets in CDs, then we suggest you re-read this book and meet us back here in an hour or so. Suffice it to say that we cannot foresee a time when taxable interest rates that are less than inflation will ever be a good decision in the light of other options like an LSA or FIA.

In the risk-exposed tank (RV), some amounts of money exposed to unlimited loss and gains can sometimes be tolerated. It has historically been suggested in financial planning advice to limit this amount to no more than 20% of your total savings amounts. Additionally, as with any other gamble, if you cannot afford to lose it all, then do not put it there. Another consideration is that this percentage usually decreases as you get older. The "rule of 100" dictates that as you get closer to retirement age you will have less and less time to recover from losses, so an increasing portion of your money should be transferred away from market risks into a tank that is safe and protected from losses.

The Future Proof tank (FP) is where you will put your LSA and FIA investment dollars. As stated earlier, do not worry yet about how much will be in an LSA or how much will go into an FIA. For now, just maximize this tank percentage to the percentage of your total financial picture that you feel comfortable with.

Sometimes, the easiest way to fill in all three

TYPICAL DESIRED FUTURE PROOF ALLOCATIONS MIX

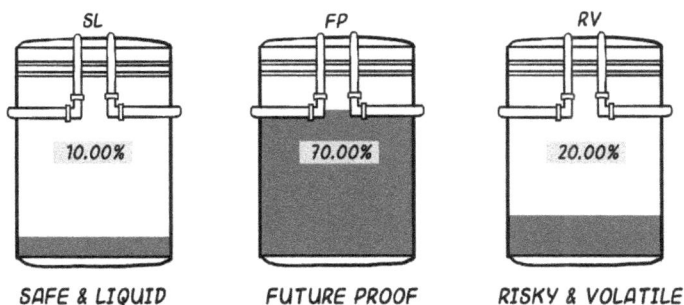

SL	FP	RV
10.00%	70.00%	20.00%
SAFE & LIQUID	FUTURE PROOF	RISKY & VOLATILE

percentages is to put your desired percentage in the banking tank, decide the percentage you will leave in the risky and volatile tank, and then put the remainder into the center, Future Proof tank.

Now that we have your three desired percentages, let's examine what your current state is. For this step, list all of your retirement and investment assets on a piece of paper with dollar amounts o the side, then add up the assets for the total amount investable. Then for each individual asset, determine whether it is currently a tank one, two, or three asset and write that corresponding dollar amount in that column.

Once all your assets have been placed in their corresponding tanks, add up each tank subtotal. To calculate the percentages of each current tank amount,

TYPICAL ACTUAL ALLOCATIONS MIX

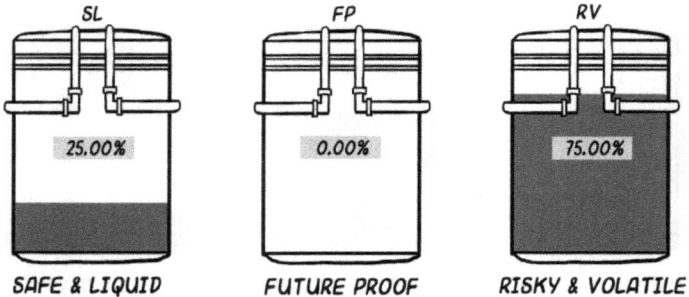

SL	FP	RV
25.00%	0.00%	75.00%
SAFE & LIQUID	FUTURE PROOF	RISKY & VOLATILE

divide the subtotals of each tank by the total amount investable and multiply the result by one hundred. Write these numbers at the bottom of each corresponding tank. These numbers are the current percentage allocations of your portfolio.

Now comes the fun part. Compare your current percentages from step two to your desired percentages from step one. Is there a difference? Most first timers

DOES "WHAT YOU HAVE" = "WHAT YOU WANT"?

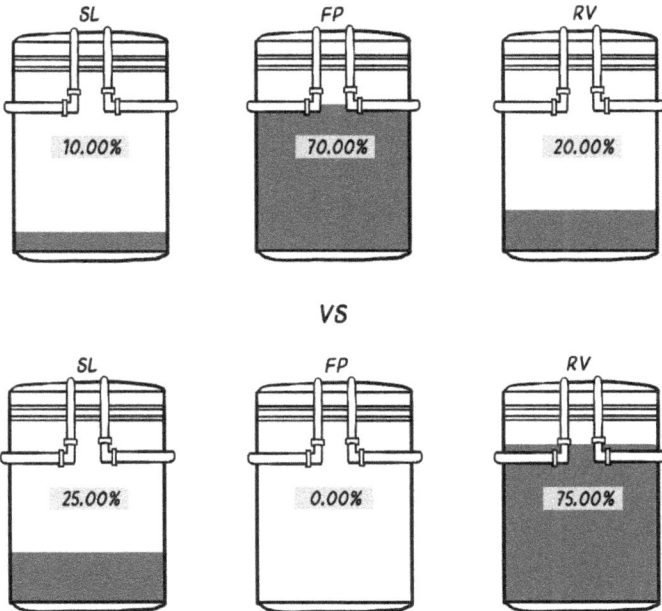

SL	FP	RV
10.00%	70.00%	20.00%

VS

SL	FP	RV
25.00%	0.00%	75.00%

find a very large discrepancy at this point. Don't feel bad if there is—feel excited that you discovered it now. As we all know, admitting you have a problem is the first step on the path to correcting it.

Now comes the somewhat trickier part. Again, if you attend one of our workshops we will lead you through this, and it is much easier to show than it is to explain.

Most people realize that they have all their assets exclusively in the banking tank and risky and volatile tank, but they desire to have a larger percentage in the center Future Proof tank. This creates the need to begin planning proper allocation movements from the right and left into the center. This is where a qualified Future Proof advisor is critical. You should not be too hasty here; before you move anything, employ a qualified future proof coach and advisor to evaluate which assets have possible strings that may need to be cut before moving them over. It is very important that each asset be individually evaluated before movement is initiated. In our workshops we walk students through these concerns and set them up for success.

It is important to note that Future Proof advisors do not necessarily want to replace your stockbroker or your banker. If you already have one of those, you can decide to keep them—just don't expect them to be very happy that you have educated yourself and are re-allocating your total portfolio. Be prepared to assure them that it will all be fine and to breathe naturally while they rant and spew their usual litany of Ford-salesman-versus-Chevy-salesman fear, uncertainty, and doubt. Or you may choose to do as our good friend's website suggests www.fireyourbrokerandbanker.com, and ask your Future Proof advisor to suggest a new resource or two.

Now let's move to step three: balancing the Future Proof tank allocation. The center tank is an LSA and FIA combination. Since this column is not exposed to market risks, there is no need to mandate a 50/50 split like you were told in the 4% rule. In this column, the balancing act is determined by time and liquidity concerns. If you are very close to retirement, then filling FIAs with as much money as you can as early as you can may be your top priority. FIAs can provide excellent growth in the first year, whereas an LSA is more of a slow starter that builds to be a big hitter later. But remember the Old Brain: it wants liquidity, and that is always an emotional decision, as the LSA is what creates the liquidity from this tank.

Chapter 8: Mission Planning

But no matter what level of liquidity you decide upon, there are two primary ways to fund your LSAs. One is through a large lump sum premium installment, and the other is to start small and build it consistently. The lump sum and large upfront installments grow the fastest. They prime the compound interest pump early, creating the best long-term performance. But not everyone has large lump sums to put into their LSA accounts. Some will simply put in the largest annual amounts they can for the first five to seven years, creating a fully-funded LSA that is ready to go. Others plan on smaller, incremental annual or monthly payments to grow their LSA like a savings account on steroids throughout their pre-retirement years. Either way, it is best to fund an LSA as quickly as you possibly can for the best results.

Since there are no set percentages for your LSA and FIA allocations, calling your Future Proof investments a "balanced portfolio" is not accurate. The center column portfolio is proportioned based on your liquidity desires and your growth needs. Once you have created the right mix for you, we call this your "Proportioned Portfolio.

Congratulations! Now you have the mission plan you desire to Future Proof your retirement investments and savings.

GLOSSARY OF TERMS

4% Draw Down Rule: a rule of thumb used to determine the amount of funds to withdraw from a retirement account each year. The 4% rule seeks to provide a steady stream of funds to the retiree, while also keeping an account balance that will allow funds to be withdrawn for a number of years. The 4% rate is considered to be a "safe" rate with the withdrawals consisting primarily of interest and dividends. The withdraw rate is kept constant, though it can be increased to keep pace with inflation.

401(k): a 401(k) plan set up for an individual running a sole proprietorship or a small business with a spouse/ immediate family member. Plan contribution limits for the individual are equal to a typical company-sponsored 401(k), but the sole proprietor can also make an employer contribution to an independent 401(k), thereby raising the total contribution allowed. The independent 401(k) may also be called a "solo 401(k)" or an "indie K."

403(b): The features of a 403(b) plan are very similar to those of a 401(k) plan. Employees may make salary deferral contributions that are usually limited by regulatory caps. Individual accounts in a 403(b) plan can be any of the following types:

- An annuity contract, which is provided through an insurance company

- A custodial account, which is invested in mutual funds

- A retirement income account set up for church employees

Accumulation: the amount one has in dollar value in an investment account.

Accumulation Value: accumulation units are used to accurately measure the value of contributions by the annuitant. In times when the variable annuity's investments dip, a fixed amount of funds will buy more accumulation units than when the securities are more highly priced, just as investors are able to buy more shares of cheaper stock than they can of higher-priced stock with the same amount of currency.

Aggressive Investing: committing money to earn a financial return with willingness to risk 100% of your principal.

Alpha: one of five technical risk ratios. Simply stated, alpha is often considered to represent the value that a portfolio manager adds to or subtracts from a fund's return. A positive alpha of 1 means the fund has outperformed its benchmark index by 1%. Correspondingly, a similar negative alpha would indicate an underperformance of 1%.

Annuity: a financial instrument that provides a stream of payments for a predetermined number of years. An annuity certain will continue a stream of payments remitted to the annuitant's beneficiary or estate, if the annuitant dies before the payment term ends. The payments are made on a regular schedule, such as monthly, quarterly, semiannually, or annually.

Balanced Portfolio: an investment portfolio that holds a mix of different types of investments, such as bonds, shares in companies, and mutual funds.

Glossary of Terms

Bank: an establishment for the custody, loan, exchange, or issue of money, for the extension of credit, and for facilitating the transmission of funds.

Bear Market: a market condition in which the prices of securities are falling, and widespread pessimism causes the negative sentiment to be self-sustaining. As investors anticipate losses in a bear market and selling continues, pessimism only grows. Although figures can vary, for many, a downturn of 20% or more in multiple broad market indexes, such as the Dow Jones Industrial Average (DJIA) or Standard & Poor's 500 Index (S&P 500), over at least a two-month period, is considered an entry into a bear market.

Beta: one of five technical risk ratios. Beta is calculated using regression analysis, and you can think of beta as the tendency of a security's returns to respond to swings in the market. A beta of 1 indicates that the security's price will move with the market. A beta of less than 1 means that the security will be less volatile than the market. A beta of greater than 1 indicates that the security's price will be more volatile than the market. For example, if a stock's beta is 1.2, it's theoretically 20% more volatile than the market. Many utilities stocks have a beta of less than 1. Conversely, most high-tech, Nasdaq-based stocks have a beta of greater than 1, offering the possibility of a higher rate of return, but also posing more risk.

Bond: an official document in which a government or company promises to pay back an amount of money that it has borrowed and to pay interest on the borrowed money.

Bond Type Risk: each bond faces 6 or more risk issues: Types of Fixed Income Risk, Mathematical Explanation for Interest Rate Risk, Supply and Demand Explanation for Interest Rate Risk, the Real World Implication of Interest Rate Risk, and the Bottom Line. So what are the implications of investing in fixed income securities in a fluctuating interest rate environment? First, if you plan on buying a bond and holding it until maturity, you should not worry about interest rate risk, but instead focus on default risk. Second, if you plan on buying a bond and trading it before it matures, you should buy a bond with a higher coupon rate and shorter term-to-maturity. The reason for this recommendation is that a bond with these types of features will not be as adversely affected by a rising interest rate environment. Of course, you should keep in mind that a bond that offers a higher coupon rate will likely have more default risk than a bond with a lower coupon rate. Third, you can purchase a floating rate bond in order to minimize or eliminate the impact of interest rate risk. Finally, as a bond investor, you need to determine beforehand if your goal for buying a bond is to generate income via periodic coupon payments, or if you are purchasing the bond with the expectation of receiving periodic coupon payments, as well as a material capital gain associated with the fluctuating price of the bond. If periodic income is your focus, you should concentrate on purchasing high coupon paying bonds that have a lower probability of default risk. On the other hand, if capital gains are your primary focus of interest, it is recommended that you greatly enhance your knowledge of fixed income and the global capital markets before trying to engage in such investment strategies.

Bull Market: a financial market of a group of securities in which prices are rising or are expected to rise. The term "bull market" is most often used to refer to the stock market, but can be applied to anything that is traded, such as bonds, currencies, and commodities.

Buy and Hold Management: The objective of buy and hold is to buy the initial allocation mix and then hold it indefinitely, without rebalancing, regardless of performance. There are a variety of ways to do this.

The asset allocation is allowed to vary significantly from the starting allocation as risky assets, such as stocks, increase or decrease. Buy-hold is essentially a "do not rebalance" strategy and a truly passive strategy. The portfolio becomes more aggressive as stocks rise and you let the profits ride, no matter how high the stock value gets. The portfolio becomes more defensive as stocks fall and you let the bond position become a greater percentage of the account. At some point, the value of the stocks could reach zero, leaving only bonds in the account. Most professionals working with retirement clients follow the constant mix rebalancing strategy. Most of the general investing public has no rebalancing strategy or follows buy-hold out of default rather than a conscious portfolio management strategy. Regardless of the strategy you use, in difficult economic times, you will often hear the mantra "stick to the plan," which is preceded by "be sure you have good plan." A clearly defined rebalancing strategy is a critical component of portfolio management.

Cash Reserves: in finance, cash reserves primarily refers to two things. One is a type of short-term, highly liquid investment that earns a low rate of return (perhaps 3% annually). This is where some individuals keep money that they want to have quick access to. The other type of cash reserves refers to the money a company or individual keeps on hand to meet its short-term and emergency funding needs.

Certificate of Deposit: a savings certificate entitling the bearer to receive interest. A CD bears a maturity date and a specified fixed interest rate, and it can be issued in any denomination. CDs are generally issued by commercial banks and are insured by the FDIC. The term of a CD generally ranges from one month to five years.

Collateral Capacity: cash value amount - reserve amount - outstanding lien amounts = current collateral capacity

Collateral: property or other assets that a borrower offers a lender to secure a loan. If the borrower stops making the promised loan payments, the lender can seize the collateral to recoup its losses. Because collateral offers some security to the lender in case the borrower fails to pay back the loan, loans that are secured by collateral typically have lower interest rates than unsecured loans. A lender's claim to a borrower's collateral is called a lien.

Compound Interest: interest that accrues on the initial principal and the accumulated interest of a principal deposit, loan, or debt. Compounding of interest allows a principal amount to grow at a faster rate than simple interest, which is calculated as a percentage of only the principal amount.

Conservative Investing: committing money to earn a financial return with little to no risk of your principal.

Current Surrender Value: the sum of money an insurance company will pay to the policyholder or annuity holder in the event his or her policy is voluntarily terminated before its maturity or the insured event occurs.

Distribution: the amount of cash flow received or paid out by an annuity, REIT, or other similar income-paying instrument. The distribution of a security is calculated by dividing the distributions paid (yearly, monthly, etc.) by its cost or net asset value. Distribution yield can be used as a measure of investment cash flow provided by an investment relative to the cost paid for that investment.

Diversification: balancing (as with an investment portfolio) defensively by dividing funds among securities of different industries or of different classes.

Glossary of Terms

Financial Advisor: a professional who helps individuals manage their finances by providing advice on money issues such as investments, insurance, mortgages, college savings, estate planning, taxes, and retirement, depending on what the client requests. Some financial advisors are paid a flat fee for their advice, while others earn commissions from the investments they sell to their clients.

Fixed Annuity: an insurance contract in which the insurance company makes fixed dollar payments to the annuitant for the term of the contract, usually until the annuitant dies. The insurance company guarantees both earnings and principal. A good financial instrument for those looking to receive a fixed investment income for a period of time or for one's life.

Fixed Indexed Annuity (FIA): a special class of annuities that yields returns on your contributions based on a specified equity-based index.

Fixed Principle Assets: tangible assets that an individual or company owns and uses in the production of its income and is not expected to be consumed.

Gamble: to risk losing (something valuable or important) in order to do or achieve something.

Guaranteed Minimum Surrender Value: a minimum account value based on a minimum amount of interest earned.

Income Account Value: a measure or unit used to calculate a determined value of an annuity owner's lifetime income account value, which is determined by individual companies' annuity contracts. This is either simple or compound interest based on a fixed percentage.

Indexed Annuity: a special class of annuities that yields returns on your contributions based on a specified equity-based index. These annuities can be purchased from an insurance company, and similar to other types of annuities, the terms and conditions associated with payouts will depend on what is stated in the original annuity contract.

Insurance: an agreement in which a person makes regular payments to a company and the company promises to pay money if the person is injured or dies, or to pay money equal to the value of something (such as a house or car) if it is damaged, lost, or stolen.

Interest: Interest is charged by lenders as compensation for the loss of the asset's use. In the case of lending money, the lender could have invested the funds instead of lending them out. With lending a large asset, the lender may have been able to generate income from the asset should they have decided to use it themselves. Using the simple interest formula *Simple Interest = P (principal) x I (annual interest rate) x N (years)*, borrowing $1,000 at a 6% annual interest rate for eight months means that you would owe $40 in interest ($1,000 x 6% x 8/12). Using the compound interest formula *Compound Interest = P (principal) x [(1 + I (interest rate) N (months)) - 1]*, borrowing $1,000 at a 6% annual interest rate for 8 months means that you would owe $40.70. The interest owed when compounding is taken into consideration is higher, because interest has been charged monthly on the principal, plus accrued interest from the previous months. For shorter time frames, the calculation of interest will be similar for both methods. As the lending time increases, however, the disparity between the two types of interest calculations grows.

Investing: committing money in order to earn a financial return.

Investing Paradigm: a model or pattern for investing that may be copied.

IRA: an individual retirement account that allows individuals to direct pretax income, up to specific annual limits, toward investments that can grow tax-deferred (no capital gains or dividend income is taxed). Individual taxpayers are allowed to contribute 100% of compensation up to a specified maximum dollar amount to their traditional IRA. Contributions to the traditional IRA may be tax-deductible depending on the taxpayer's income, tax-filing status, and other factors. Other variants of the IRA include the Roth IRA, SIMPLE IRA and SEP IRA. All distributions from IRA's usually are considered taxable in the form of ordinary income.

Life Insurance: a type of insurance that pays money to the family of someone who has died.

Life Savings Account (LSA): a specifically designed life insurance policy that follows IRS tax laws to qualify as a maximum-funded contract that performs at a level that is superior to a general insurance design.

Liquid: consisting of or capable of ready conversion into cash.

Maximum Efficiency Contract: an insurance contract that has been designed to offer maximum benefits to the policy holder.

Moderate Investing: committing money to earn a financial return with a willingness to risk a small portion of your principal.

Modified Endowment Contract (MEC): In a general sense, the corridor rule states that in order for any life insurance policy to avoid being classified as a MEC, there must be a "corridor" of difference in dollar value between the death benefit and the cash value of the policy. All single-premium policies are now classified as MECs. Flexible premium policies must pass the seven-pay test in order to avoid MEC status. This test caps the amount of premium that can be paid into a flexible premium policy over a period of seven years. While this states that you must use seven years, this can be a shorter timeline based on deeper understanding of the corridor.

Money Market Accounts: savings accounts that offer the competitive rate of interest (real rate) in exchange for larger-than-normal deposits.

Mutual Fund: a type of investment in which the money of many people is used to buy stock from many different companies.

Permanent Life Insurance: an umbrella term for life insurance plans that do not expire (unlike term life insurance) and combine a death benefit with a savings portion. This savings portion can build a cash value against which the policy owner can borrow funds, or in some instances, the owner can withdraw the cash value to help meet future goals, such as paying for a child's college education. The two main types of permanent life insurance are whole and universal life insurance policies.

Portfolio: the total investments that are owned by a person or organization.

Prudent Rules: A prudent investment will not always turn out to be a good investment, because no one can predict with certainty what will happen with any investment decision. Thus, the rule only applies to the decision-making process; that is, based on the knowledge the fiduciary has at the time, is the investment a good idea? Investing exclusively in penny stocks, for example, would violate the prudent investor rule, because they are known to be risky at the outset.

Real Estate: land plus anything permanently fixed to it, including buildings, sheds, and other items attached to the structure. Though the media often refers to the "real estate market" from the perspective of residential living, real estate can be grouped into three broad categories based on its use: residential, commercial, and industrial. Examples of real estate include undeveloped land, houses, condominiums, town homes, office buildings, retail store buildings, and factories.

Required Minimum Distributions: These required minimum distributions are determined by dividing the prior year-end fair market value of the retirement account by the applicable distribution period or life expectancy. Some qualified plans will allow certain participants to defer beginning their RMDs until they retire, even if they are older than age seventy and a half. Qualified plan participants should check with their employers to determine whether they are eligible for this deferral.

Retirement: Dramatic advances in healthcare have extended the lives of people in, predominantly, first-world and developed countries. That means that without adequate personal savings and/or pensions, people could easily outlive their retirement funds. In times of economic downturn retirees may choose to "come out of retirement" and re-enter the workforce on a seasonal, part-time, or full-time basis to earn income and obtain benefits, especially costly health insurance coverage.

Reward: something that is given in return for risk.

Risk: the possibility of loss.

Risk Tolerance: a scale used to determine one's openness to risk.

R-Squared: one of five technical risk ratios. R-squared values range from 0 to 100. An R-squared of 100 means that all movements of a security are completely explained by movements in the index. A high R-squared (between 85 and 100) indicates the fund's performance patterns have been in line with the index. A fund with a low R-squared (70 or less) doesn't act much like the index. A higher R-squared value will indicate a more useful beta figure. For example, if a fund has an R-squared value of close to 100 but has a beta below 1, it is most likely offering higher risk-adjusted returns. A low R-squared means you should ignore the beta.

Safety: the state of being secure from harm, danger, and loss.

Savings: according to Keynesian economics, the amount left over when the cost of a person's consumer expenditure is subtracted from the amount of disposable income that he or she earns in a given period of time.

Standard Deviation: one of five technical risk ratios. Standard deviation is a statistical measurement that sheds light on historical volatility. For example, a volatile stock will have a high standard deviation while the deviation of a stable blue chip stock will be lower. A large dispersion tells us how much the return on the fund is deviating from the expected normal returns.

Stock: a share of the value of a company which can be bought, sold, or traded as an investment.

Stock Type Risk: each stock faces ten types of risk: Commodity Price Risk, Headline Risk, Rating Risk, Obsolescence Risk, Detection Risk, Legislative Risk, Inflationary Risk, Interest Rate Risk, Model Risk, and the Bottom Line. There is no such thing as a risk-free stock or business. Although every stock faces these universal risks and additional risks specific to their business, the rewards of investing can still far outweigh them. As an investor, the best thing you can do is to know the risks before you buy in, and perhaps keep a bottle of whiskey and a stress ball nearby during periods of market turmoil.

Stretch Plans: Stretching out an IRA gives the funds in the IRA more time—potentially decades—to compound tax-deferred. This provides the opportunity to grow the funds significantly for future generations. With a traditional IRA, the owner has to begin taking the required minimum distribution (RMD) by April 1 of the year after turning seventy and a half. The RMD is calculated by taking the account balance on December 31 of the previous year and dividing that number by the number of years left in the owner's life expectancy (as listed in the IRS's Uniform Lifetime table). Each year, the RMD is calculated by dividing the account balance by the remaining life expectancy. Non-spousal heirs of any age, regardless of the type of IRA, must take RMDs based on their life expectancy. The younger the beneficiary the lower the RMD, which allows more funds to remain in the IRA to stretch the IRA over time. However, not all IRAs allow the stretch strategy, and investors should check with their provider or financial institution to determine if beneficiaries will be allowed to take distributions over a life expectancy period.

Systematic Risk: interest rates, recession, and wars all represent sources of systematic risk because they affect the entire market and cannot be avoided through diversification. Whereas this type of risk affects a broad range of securities, unsystematic risk affects a very specific group of securities or an individual security. Systematic risk can be mitigated only by being hedged. Even a portfolio of well-diversified assets cannot escape all risk.

Tactical Management: What makes tactical investing strategies so popular? Is it the triumph of hope over reality? Is it a reflection of our digital, instant-news society bleeding over into the investment world and selling the idea of "instant" trading, even though that rarely happens? Or perhaps it's the psychological need to feel like you can take action when the financial markets decline. Whatever the answer, these strategies continue to grow in popularity and continue to attract assets as well, bucking the larger trend away from active management.

Technical Risk Ratios: The five technical risk rations (alpha, beta, standard deviation, R-squared, and the Sharpe ratio) are all statistical measurements used in modern portfolio theory (MPT). All five indicators are intended to help investors determine the risk-reward profile of a mutual fund.

Transfer: a change in ownership of an asset, or a movement of funds and/or assets from one account to another. A transfer may involve an exchange of funds when it involves a change in ownership, such as when an investor sells a real estate holding. In this case, there is a transfer of title from the seller to the buyer and a simultaneous transfer of funds, equal to the negotiated price, from the buyer to the seller. The term transfer may also refer to the movement of an account from one bank or brokerage to another.

Variable Annuity: the portfolio generally invests in equity securities and mutual funds, and its performance determines the amount of this total payment. This has market risk associated with the investment options, along with additional cost to the owner.

Variance: a measure of the variability (volatility) from an average. Volatility is a measure of risk, so this statistic can help determine the risk an investor might take on when purchasing a specific security.

Volatility: the amount of uncertainty or risk about the size of changes in a security's value. A higher volatility means that a security's value can potentially be spread out over a larger range of values. This means that the price of the security can change dramatically over a short time period in either direction. A lower volatility means that a security's value does not fluctuate dramatically, but changes in value at a steady pace over a period of time. Volatility can either be measured by using the standard deviation or variance between returns from that same security or market index.

Resources

Bengen, William P. "Determining Withdrwal Rates
Using Historical Data." *Journal of Financial
Planning* (October 1994): 171-180.

Blanchett, David M., Finke, Michael, and Wade D. Pfau.
"The 4% Rule is Not Safe in a Low-Yield World."
Journal of Financial Planning.

Fleck, Colin. "Running Out of Money Worse Than
Death." *AARP Bulletin*, July 1, 2010.

Jamieson, Dan. "Finra warns on bonds." *Investment
News*, February 14, 2013.

McMahon, Tim. "Historical Inflation Rate."
InflationData.com, November 20, 2013.

Pfau, Wade D. "Fees and sustainable retirement

income." *Wall Street Journal: Market Watch,*
March 20, 2013.

Pfau, Wade D. "An International Perspective on Safe
Withdrawal Rates: The Demise of the 4 Percent
Rule?" *Journal of Financial Planning.*

Scott, Jason S., Sharpe, William F., and John G.
Watson. "The 4% Rule—At What Price?" *Journal of
Investment Management* 7, no. 3 (2009): 31-48.

Society of Actuaries. "2011 Risks and Process of
Retirement Survey Report: Key Findings and
Issues: Longevity." June 2012.

ABOUT THE AUTHORS

Kelly Gilbert spent over twenty years in small business and process improvement consulting before co-founding Eminence Financial. Kelly has taught and trained on such topics as late-term college funding, cash flow optimization, lifetime income arbitrage, asset optimization, indexed and charitable gift annuities, infinite banking, qualified retirement plan alternatives, tax shelter strategies, and advanced insurance management techniques. Kelly's passion is providing awareness of these advanced strategies to those who were previously never given access to them, namely the millions of small business owners and upper middle class Americans who have been hurt so badly by the traditional and mass-produced financial services advice.

Steve Kitchen, partner and COO with the Eminence Group, specializes in working with business owners, professionals, pre-retirees, and post-retirees. He is also highly focused on working with the top college funding experts in the country to help you and your children get the best college education you can afford. Steve has trained CPAs, attorneys, and financial planners. As an accomplished keynote speaker, Steve has been featured in many events speaking on retirement after work, income planning, college planning, and Social Security. He has also been featured on AnnuityNewsNow and RetirementNewsToday. Steve and his wife Julie have three children, Haley, Hillary, and Riley.